Bread
Machines
& beyond

Bread
Machines
& beyond

Jennie Shapter

southwater

This edition published in 2001 by Southwater

Distributed in the UK by
The Manning Partnership
251-253 London Road East
Batheaston, Bath BA1 7RL, UK
tel. (0044) 01225 852 727
fax. (0044) 01225 852 852

Distributed in the USA by
Ottenheimer Publishing
5 Park Center Court, Suite 300
Owing Mills MD 2117-5001, USA
tel. (001) 410 902 9100
fax. (001) 410 902 7210

Distributed in Australia by
Sandstone Publishing
Unit 1, 360 Norton Street, Leichhardt,
New South Wales 2040, Australia
tel. (0061) 2 9560 7888
fax. (0061) 2 9560 7488

Distributed in Canada by
Anness Publishing
c/o Raincoast Book Distributors
8680 Cambie Street
Vancouver BC V6P 6M9, Canada
tel. (001) 604 323 7100
fax. (001) 604 323 7109

Distributed in New Zealand by
Five Mile Press NZ
Unit 3/46a Taharoto Road
PO Box 33-1071
Takapuna
Auckland 9
New Zealand
tel. (0064) 9 486 1925
fax. (0064) 9 486 1454

Southwater is an imprint of Anness Publishing Limited. ©2001/2002 Anness Publishing Limited

3 5 7 9 10 8 6 4

PUBLISHER: Joanna Lorenz
MANAGING EDITOR: Helen Sudell
EDITOR: Debra Mayhew
DESIGNER: Nigel Partridge
PHOTOGRAPHER AND STYLIST: Nicki Dowey
HOME ECONOMIST: Jennie Shapter
PRODUCTION CONTROLLER: Joanna King

Previously published as part of a larger compendium, The Ultimate Bread Machine Cookbook

NOTES

Bracketed terms are intended for American readers. American terms are only given in the list of ingredients for the small
size of bread machine: please refer to this ingredients list if you are making bread in a larger machine.

The recipes in this book have all been written and tested for use in a variety of bread machines available from
leading manufacturers. For best results, refer to your manufacturer's handbook to confirm the proportion of flour to liquids.
You may need to adjust the recipes to suit your machine.

For all recipes, quantities are given in both metric and imperial measures and, where appropriate, measures are also given in
standard cups and spoons. Follow one set, but not a mixture, because they are not interchangeable.Standard spoon and cup
measures are level.1 tsp = 5ml, 1 tbsp = 15 ml, 1 cup = 250ml/8fl oz. Australian standard tablespoons are 20ml. Australian
readers should use 3 tsp in place of 1 tbsp for measuring small quantities of ingredients.

Medium eggs (US large) are used unless otherwise stated.

CONTENTS

INTRODUCTION

—

There are few things more appetizing than the aroma of freshly baked bread, and a basket full of home-made rolls makes any supper table seem really special. However, the laborious process of mixing, kneading and waiting for the dough to rise, sometimes twice, doesn't combine easily with today's busy lifestyle. Home baking was fast becoming a thing of the past – part of an idyllic childhood and a fantasy farmhouse kitchen – when the first bread machine appeared on the market in the late 1980s. These excellent appliances have helped to rekindle the pleasure of making bread at home by streamlining the process and making it incredibly simple. All the home baker needs to do is to measure a few ingredients accurately, put them into the bread machine pan and push a button or two.

INGREDIENT LISTS

At first sight, all the settings on the control panel of a modern bread machine can be a little overwhelming, but they are

BELOW: What could be a more delicious breakfast than toasted, home-baked Buttermilk Bread?

there to help you bake a wide range of different types of bread, whether sweet or savoury, using a variety of grains and flavourings. Start by making a basic white loaf and watch while your machine transforms simple and inexpensive ingredients first into a silky smooth dough and finally into crisp, golden bread. Before long, you will be so familiar with your machine that ciabatta and sourdoughs, breadsticks and yeast cakes will feature on your family menus as a matter of routine.

The breads in this book are made entirely by machine or the dough is made in the machine, then shaped by hand and baked in a conventional oven. Teabreads are mixed by hand and baked in the bread machine. Where the loaves are made automatically, you will usually find three separate lists of ingredients, each list relating to a different size of machine. The small size is recommended for machines that are designed for loaves using 350–375g/12–13oz/3–3¼ cups flour, the medium size for machines that make loaves using 450-500g/1lb-1¼lb/4-4½ cups flour, and the large size for bread machines that are capable of making loaves using up to 675g/1½lb/6 cups flour.

ABOVE: Add mixed seeds to the dough for Four Seed Bread to give a tasty and nutritious crunch to the loaf.

Refer to the manufacturer's handbook if you are unsure of the capacity of your machine. If only one set of ingredients are given for a loaf that is to be baked automatically, check the size of your machine to make sure it is suitable for the job. Where a bread machine is used only for preparing the dough, which is then shaped by hand and baked conventionally, quantities are not so crucial and only one set of ingredients is given.

THE HUMAN TOUCH

Whatever type of bread machine you have, focus on the bread rather than the machine. It is a kitchen aid and can only do what you programme it to do. It is essential to add the correct ingredients in the right proportions in the order specified in the manufacturer's instructions. Choose the right setting and the machine will mix, knead and bake beautifully. As you get to know your machine and begin to experiment, you will quickly learn how to make the perfect loaf and how to compensate for those variables, such as the humidity and the weather, over which no one has any control.

When you make bread by hand, you can feel if the dough is too wet or too dry as you knead it, but you cannot do this with a bread machine. Instead, check the dough after a few minutes' mixing in the machine to see if it is pliable and soft. When the machine stops kneading, the

dough should start to relax back into the shape of the pan. You will quickly learn to recognize when the dough is the right consistency and in no time at all you will be making loaves with different flours, such as wholemeal (whole-wheat) and rye, and flavoured with vegetables, such as spinach and courgettes (zucchini). The range of both savoury and sweet breads you ultimately will be able to produce will be limited only by your imagination.

AN AMAZING RANGE

The recipes in this book are divided into five chapters. The first covers easy-to-make, basic breads. Many of these are perfect for breakfast, freshly baked or toasted, and can also be used for sandwiches and snacks. These types of bread are the easiest to make in your machine and are the ones you are likely to make over and over again. This initial chapter also includes wonderful speciality grain loaves, such as New England Anadama Bread, made from a blend of white and wholemeal flours, and polenta. These flavour-packed breads are not only really delicious but, as a bonus, they are healthy options with added fibre.

The recipes in the second chapter show you how to take full advantage of the "dough only" setting on your machine to make an impressive selection of flatbreads as accompaniments to family

BELOW: Pizza bases can be made in the bread machine then hand-shaped and oven-baked. Top with whatever whets your appetite.

ABOVE: Mix the dough for these Mixed Grain Onion Rolls in your bread machine, then shape them by hand and bake in a conventional oven.

meals. From Indian Naan to Middle Eastern Lavash, the machine will mix the dough perfectly for you to shape by hand and then bake in a conventional oven. This chapter also includes a choice of fabulous home-made pizzas from Sicilian *Sfincione* to French *Pissaladière*.

The bread machine provides the perfect environment for sourdough and other starter-dough breads, which are the subject of the third chapter. A lengthy process of fermentation gives these loaves a characteristic tanginess and they often have a distinctive texture. These popular rustic breads are made throughout France and Italy, but for a truly unique flavour, try San Francisco-style Sourdough. As it depends on airborne yeast spores as a raising agent, rather than baker's yeast, each loaf tastes slightly different depending on where it was baked.

With the recipes in the fourth chapter you can discover how amazingly versatile your bread machine is. It will happily incorporate all kinds of ingredients, such as caramelized onions, crumbled cheese, herbs, tomatoes, and even mushrooms, to make mouth-watering savoury breads and rolls. Serve Salami and Peppercorn Bread with a steaming bowl of soup for a satisfying and flavoursome lunch or delight your guests with pretty little Spanish Picos with their pre-dinner drinks.

Sweet yeast doughs also work well in a bread machine. It is ideal for mixing the rich dough for special-occasion confections, such as Peach Brandy Babas and Finnish Festive Wreath, taking much of the hard work out of entertaining. You can also use your bread machine to cook succulent teabreads, Honey Cake, Madeira Cake and Passion Cake – to name but a few – as an alternative to heating a traditional oven for baking a single cake.

A useful introductory section offers easy-to-follow advice on how to make the most of your bread machine to achieve perfect results every time. Hints and tips throughout the book provide a wealth of variations and ideas to inspire you.

Home baking has never been so easy, so much fun or so varied. You will never want to buy another loaf again.

HOW TO USE YOUR BREAD MACHINE

All bread machines work on the same basic principle. Each contains a removable, non-stick bread pan with a handle, into which a kneading blade is fitted. When inserted into the machine, the pan fits on to a central shaft that rotates the blade. A lid closes over the bread pan so that the ingredients are contained within a controlled environment. The lid has an air vent and may have a window. The machine is programmed by the control panel.

The size and shape of the bread is determined by the shape of the bread pan. Both rectangular and square shapes are available. The former produces the more traditional shape, the specific size varying from one manufacturer to another. The square shape is mostly to be found in smaller machines and produces a tall loaf, that resembles a traditional rectangular loaf but standing on end. This can be turned on its side for slicing, if you prefer smaller slices of bread.

The following guidelines apply to any bread machine and should always be read in conjunction with the handbook provided with your particular model. Finally, make sure you use fresh, top quality ingredients to ensure good results.

ABOVE: Your bread machine can be used to make rich and tasty sweet-breads, such as this Mocha Panettone.

SPECIAL FEATURES

Extra programmes can be found on more expensive machines. These include making pasta dough and cooking jam or rice. While these facilities would not be the main reason for buying a bread machine, they can be useful extras. For instance, jam-making couldn't be easier: you simply add equal quantities of fresh fruit and sugar to the bread machine pan, set the jam programme and, when the cycle ends, you will have jam ready to pour into clean, sterilized jars.

BASIC CONTROLS

If you have a set of electronic scales with an add and weigh facility, then accurate measuring of ingredients is very easy. Stand the bread pan on the scale, pour in the liquid, then set the display to zero. Add the dry ingredients directly to the pan, each time zeroing the display. Finally, add the fat, salt, sweetener and yeast and place the bread pan in the machine.

1 Stand the bread machine on a firm, level, heat-resistant surface. Place it well away from a heat source, such as an oven, and in neither direct sunlight nor a draught. All these factors can affect the machine's internal temperature. Do not plug it into the power socket at this stage. Open the lid and remove the bread pan by holding both sides of the handle and pulling upwards or twisting slightly, depending on the model.

2 Make sure the kneading blade and shaft are free of any breadcrumbs left behind when the machine was last used. Fit the kneading blade on the shaft in the base of the bread pan.

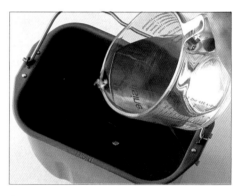

3 Pour the water, milk and/or other liquids into the bread pan, unless the manufacturer's instructions for your machine require you to add the dry ingredients first. If so, reverse the order in which you add the liquid and dry ingredients, putting the yeast in the bread pan first.

4 Sprinkle over the flour, making sure that it covers the liquid completely. Add any other dry ingredients specified in the recipe. Add the salt, sugar or honey and butter or oil, placing the four ingredients in separate corners of the pan.

5 Make a small indentation in the middle of the flour with the tip of your finger. Do not reach down as far as the liquid, otherwise the yeast will become too wet and will be activated too quickly. Remember to wipe any spillages from the outside of the bread pan.

6 Place the pan inside the machine, fitting it firmly in place. Some models have pans with a designated front and back or with clips on the outer edge which need to engage in the machine. Fold the handle down, close the lid, plug into the socket and switch on the power.

7 Select the programme you require, including crust colour and loaf size. Press Start. The kneading process will begin, unless your machine has a "rest" period to settle the temperature first.

8 Towards the end of the kneading process, the machine will beep to alert you to add any extra ingredients, such as dried fruit. Open the lid, add them if required and close the lid again.

9 At the end of the cycle, the machine will beep once more to let you know that the dough is ready or the bread is cooked. Press Stop. Open the lid of the machine. When removing baked bread, remember to use oven gloves. Avoid leaning over the machine as hot air will escape when it is opened.

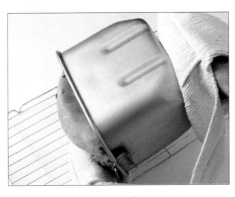

10 Turn the pan upside down and shake it several times to release the bread. If necessary, tap the base of the pan on a heatproof board. Don't try to free the bread with a knife or you will scratch the non-stick coating of the pan.

11 If the kneading blade is not a fixed one and comes out inside the bread, use a wooden spatula to remove it. It will be too hot for your fingers.

12 Place the bread on a wire rack to cool. Unplug the machine and leave it to cool before using it again. A machine that is too hot will not make a successful loaf, and, for this reason, many will not even operate if they are too hot. Leave the bread to cool for at least 30 minutes before slicing and always use a serrated knife to avoid damaging the crumb structure.

13 When the bread is cool, place it in a plastic bag or wrap it in foil and seal it. If your bread has a crisp crust, this will soften on storage so, until it is sliced, it is best left uncovered.

BASIC CONTROLS

It will take you a little while and some practice to become familiar with, and confident about using, your new bread machine. Most manufacturers produce excellent handbooks, which are supplied with their machines. The handbook is a good place to start, and should also include a "troubleshooting" section to help you if you come up against a problem. The programmes differ slightly from bread machine to bread machine, but the following overview will give you a general idea of what is involved.

START AND STOP BUTTONS

The Start button initiates the whole process. Press it after you have placed all the ingredients required for the bread-making procedure in the bread pan, positioned the pan in the machine and have selected all the necessary settings, such as loaf type, size, crust colour and delay timer.

The Stop button may be the same control or a separate one. Press it at the end of the cycle or to stop the programme if you need to override it. Pressing the Stop button cancels the "keep warm" cycle at the end of baking.

TIME DISPLAY AND STATUS INDICATOR

A window displays the time that remains until the end of the selected programme. In some machines the window also shows

SAFETY DEVICES

Most machines include a power failure override mode. If the machine is inadvertently unplugged or there is a brief power cut, the programme will continue as soon as the power is restored, up to a maximum of 10–30 minutes.

An overload protection is fitted to some models. This will cut in if the kneading blade is restricted by hard dough and will stop the motor to protect it. It will re-start after about 30 minutes. It is important to rectify the problem first.

ABOVE: The "dough only" facility is invaluable if you want to make rolls and baps.

the programme that has been selected. Some models use this window or a separate set of lights to indicate what is happening inside the machine. The window or lights give information on whether the machine is on time delay, kneading, resting, rising, baking or warming.

PROGRAMME INDICATORS OR MENU

All bread machines have a number of programmes for different types of bread, but some have more than others. Choose the appropriate programme for your recipe, such as Rapid or Whole Wheat. Most machines also include a "dough only" programme.

DELAY TIMER

Use this button to set the bread machine to switch on automatically at a specific time. This allows you to have freshly baked bread for breakfast or when you get home from work. Do not use the delay timer for dough containing perishable ingredients, such as fresh dairy products or meats.

CRUST COLOUR CONTROL

Most bread machines have a default medium crust setting. If, however, you prefer a paler crust or the appearance of a high-bake loaf, most machines give you the option of a lighter or darker crust. Breads that are high in sugar or contain eggs or cheese may colour too much on a medium setting, so a lighter option may be preferable.

WARMING INDICATOR

It is best to remove the bread from the machine as soon as it has finished baking. If for any reason this is not possible, the warming facility will switch on to help prevent condensation, which would otherwise make the bread soggy. Most machines continue in this mode for an hour, some giving an audible reminder every few minutes.

REMINDER LIGHTS

A few models are fitted with a set of lights that change colour to remind you to follow certain essential steps. This helps to make sure that the kneading blade is fitted and that basic ingredients have been placed in the bread pan.

LOAF SIZE

Larger bread machines may offer the option of making up to three different sizes of loaf. Sizes vary according to the model, but approximate to small (450g/1lb), medium (675g/1½lb) and large (900g/2lb). In some machines, this control is for visual indication only and does not alter the baking time or cycle. Check the manufacturer's handbook.

PREHEAT CYCLE

Some bread machines start all programmes with a preheat cycle, or warming phase, either before mixing or during the kneading phase. This feature is useful on colder days or when you are using large quantities of ingredients, such as milk or eggs, straight from the refrigerator.

BAKING PROGRAMMES

Different programmes allow you to vary the kneading, rising and baking times to suit different recipes and different types of flour, and to determine the texture of the finished loaf.

BASIC OR NORMAL

This is the most commonly used programme and is ideal for white loaves and mixed grain loaves where white flour is the main ingredient.

RAPID

This cycle reduces the time to make a standard loaf by about an hour. The finished loaf may not have risen so much as one on the basic programme and may be a little denser.

WHOLE WHEAT

Longer than the basic cycle, this special programme allows time for the slower rising action of doughs containing a high percentage of strong wholemeal (wholewheat) flour. Some machines also have a multigrain mode for breads made with cereals and grains, such as Granary (multi-grain) and rye. However, you can make satisfactory breads using either this or the basic mode, depending on the proportions of the flours.

FRENCH

This programme is best suited to low-fat and low-sugar breads. The rising time is longer and, in some machines, the loaf is baked at a slightly higher temperature.

SWEET BREAD

A few bread machines offer this feature in addition to crust colour control. It is useful if you intend to bake breads with a high fat or sugar content as these tend to colour too much.

CAKE

Again, this is a feature offered on a few machines. Some will mix a quick non-yeast teabread-type cake and then bake it; others will mix yeast-raised cakes.

If you do not have this facility, teabreads and non-yeast cakes can easily be mixed in a bowl and cooked in the bread pan on a "bake only" cycle.

BAKE

The bake setting allows you to use your bread machine as an oven to bake cakes and ready-prepared dough from the supermarket or to extend the standard baking time if you like your bread very well done.

SANDWICH

A very few models offer this facility for baking a loaf with a soft crust that is ideal for sandwich slices.

RAISIN BEEP

Extra ingredients can be added mid-cycle in most programmes. The machine gives an audible signal and some machines pause late in the kneading phase so that ingredients, such as dried fruit and nuts, can be added. If you do not have this facility, set a kitchen timer to ring 5 minutes before the end of the kneading phase.

DOUGH PROGRAMMES

Most machines include at least one dough programme: some models will also have dough programmes with extra features.

DOUGH

This programme is for making dough without baking it in the machine, which is essential for all hand-shaped breads. When the risen dough is ready, it can be shaped by hand, allowed to rise a second time and then baked in a conventional oven. If you wish to make different shaped loaves or rolls, you will find this facility invaluable.

OTHER DOUGH PROGRAMMES

Some machines include cycles for making different types of dough, such as a rapid dough mode for pizzas and a longer mode for wholemeal dough. Some "dough only" cycles also include the raisin beep facility.

BELOW: Sun-dried tomatoes and dried mushrooms can be added to the dough at the "raisin beep" stage to make a delicious loaf.

GETTING THE BEST FROM YOUR MACHINE

It is impossible to include all the hints and tips you will need. As you gain experience and confidence you will be able to solve more and more of any little problems that crop up. In the meantime, here are a few pointers to help you.

FOLLOW THE INSTRUCTIONS

Always add the ingredients to your bread machine in the order suggested by the manufacturer. Whatever the order, keep the yeast dry and separate from any liquids added to the bread pan.

MEASURING INGREDIENTS

Measure both the liquids and the dry ingredients carefully. More problems occur because ingredients are inaccurately measured, one ingredient is forgotten or the same ingredient is added twice. Do not exceed the quantities of flour and liquid recommended for your machine – check the handbook carefully. Mixing the extra ingredients may overload the motor and if you have too much dough, it is likely to rise over the top of the pan causing a lot of mess.

ABOVE: Always measure ingredients accurately as your bread machine cannot compensate for human error.

LEFT: The smell and taste of freshly baked bread brings back memories of childhood to many people.

WATCHING THE DOUGH

Keep a flexible rubber spatula next to the machine and, if necessary, scrape down the sides of the pan after 5–10 minutes of the initial mixing cycle. The kneading blade sometimes fails to pick up a thick or sticky dough from the corners of the pan.

CHECKING THE DOUGH

You should check the dough within the first 5 minutes of mixing, especially when you are trying a recipe for the first time. If the dough seems too wet and instead of forming a ball sticks to the sides of the pan, add a little flour, a spoonful at a time. However, the bread machine requires a dough that is slightly wetter than if you were mixing it by hand. If the dough is crumbly and won't form a ball, add liquid, one spoonful at a time. You will soon get used to the sound of the motor and notice if it is labouring owing to a stiff mix.

ABOVE: The dough is too dry and requires more water.

BELOW: The dough is too wet and requires more flour.

SAFETY

1 Read the manufacturer's advice and instructions before operating your machine. Keep any instruction manuals provided with your machine handy for future reference.

2 If you touch the machine while it is in operation, take good care. The outside walls become hot when it is in baking mode.

3 Position the machine on a firm, level, heat-resistant surface, away from any other heat source.

4 Do not stand the machine in direct sunlight and allow at least 5–7.5cm/ 2–3in clearance on all sides.

5 Do not place anything on top of the machine lid.

6 Do not use the machine outdoors.

7 Do not immerse the machine, cable or plug in water and avoid using it near a sink.

8 Be careful to keep your fingers away from the blade while the machine is kneading the dough and never reach inside the machine during the baking cycle. Do not lean over the machine when taking out baked bread.

9 Keep the machine out of the reach of young children and make sure there is no trailing cable.

10 Unplug the machine before cleaning or moving it and when it is not in use. Allow the bread machine to cool before cleaning and storing it.

HAND-SHAPING LOAVES

One of the most useful features to look out for when buying a bread machine is the dough setting. On this setting, the machine will automatically mix the ingredients and then knead and rest the dough before providing the ideal conditions for it to rise for the first time. The whole cycle, from mixing through to rising, takes about 1¾ hours.

KNOCKING BACK (PUNCHING DOWN)

1 At the end of the cycle, the dough will have almost doubled in bulk and will be ready for shaping. Remove the bread pan from the machine.

2 Lightly flour a work surface. Gently remove the dough from the pan and place it on the floured surface. Knock back (punch down) or deflate the dough to relieve the tension in the gluten and expel some of the carbon dioxide.

3 Knead the dough lightly for 1–2 minutes, then shape it into a tight ball. At this stage, a recipe may suggest covering the dough with oiled clear film (plastic wrap) or an upturned bowl and leaving it to rest for a few minutes. This allows the gluten to relax so the dough will be easier to handle.

SHAPING

Techniques to shape dough vary, depending on the finished form of the bread you wish to make. The following steps illustrate how to form basic bread, roll and yeast pastry shapes.

BAGUETTE

1 To shape a baguette or French stick, flatten the dough into a rectangle about 2.5cm/1in thick, either using the palms of your hands or a rolling pin.

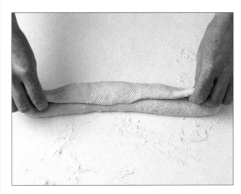

2 From one long side fold one-third of the dough down and then fold over the remaining third of dough and press gently to secure. Repeat twice more, resting the dough in between folds to avoid tearing.

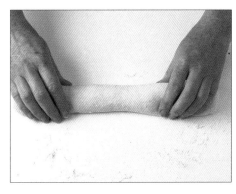

3 Gently stretch the dough and roll it backwards and forwards with your hands to make a breadstick of even thickness and the required length.

4 Place the baguette dough between a folded floured dish towel, or in a banneton, and leave in a warm place to prove. The dish towel or banneton will help the baguette to keep the correct shape as it rises.

COTTAGE LOAF

1 To shape a cottage loaf, divide the dough into two pieces, approximately one-third and two-thirds in size. Shape each piece of dough into a plump round ball and place on lightly floured baking sheets. Cover with inverted bowls and leave to rise for 30 minutes, or until 50 per cent larger.

2 Flatten the top of the large loaf. Using a sharp knife, cut a cross about 4cm/1½in across in the centre. Brush the area lightly with water and place the small round on top.

3 Using one or two fingers or the floured handle of a wooden spoon, press the centre of the top round, penetrating into the middle of the dough beneath.

TWIST

1 To shape bread for a twist, divide the dough into two equal pieces. Using the palms of your hands, roll each piece of dough on a lightly floured surface into a long rope, about 4–5cm/1½–2in thick. Make both ropes the same length.

2 Place the two ropes side by side. Starting from the centre, twist one rope over the other. Continue in the same way until you reach the end, then pinch the ends together and tuck the join underneath. Turn the dough around and repeat the process with the other end, twisting the dough in the same direction as the first.

BREADSTICK

To shape a breadstick, roll the dough to a rectangle about 1cm/½in thick, and cut out strips that are about 7.5cm/3in long and 2cm/¾in wide. Using the palm of your hand, gently roll each strip into a long thin rope.

It may help to lift each rope and pull it very gently to stretch it. If you are still finding it difficult to stretch the dough, leave it to rest for a few minutes and then try again.

COURONNE

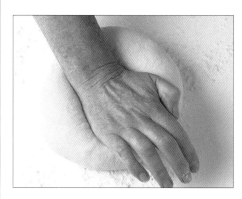

1 Shape the dough into a ball. Using the heal of your hand make a hole in the centre. Gradually enlarge the centre, turning the dough to make a circle, with a 13cm–15cm/5–6in cavity.

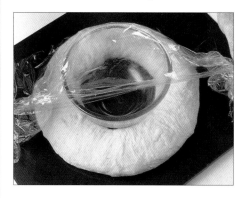

2 Place on a lightly oiled baking sheet. Put a small, lightly oiled bowl in the centre of the ring to prevent the dough from filling in the centre during rising.

SCROLL

Roll out the dough using the palms of your hands to form a rope, about 25cm/10in long, with tapered ends. Form into a loose "S" shape, then curl the ends in to make a scroll. Leave a small space to allow for the final proving (rising).

CROISSANT

1 To shape a croissant, roll out the dough on a lightly floured surface and then cut it into strips that are about 15cm/6in wide.

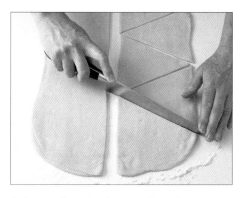

2 Cut each strip along its length into triangles with 15cm/6in bases and 18cm/7in sides.

3 Place with the pointed end towards you and the 15cm/6in base at the top; gently pull each corner of the base to stretch it slightly.

4 Roll up the dough with one hand from the base while pulling, finishing with the dough point underneath. Finally, curve the corners around in the direction of the pointed end to make the curved croissant shape.

PLAITED (BRAIDED) ROLL

1 To shape a plaited roll, place the dough on a lightly floured surface and roll out. Divide the dough into balls, the number depending on the amount of dough and how many rolls you would like to make.

2 Divide each ball of dough into three equal pieces. Using your hands, roll into long, thin ropes of equal length and place them side by side.

3 Pinch one of the ends together and plait (braid) the pieces of dough. Finally, pinch the remaining ends together and then tuck the join under.

FILLED PLAITED BRAID

1 Place the dough for the plaited braid on a lightly floured surface. Roll out and shape into a rectangle. Using a sharp knife, make diagonal cuts down each of the long sides of the dough, about 2cm/¾in wide. Place the filling in the centre of the uncut strip.

2 Fold in the end strip of dough, then fold over alternate strips of dough to form a plait over the filling. Tuck in the final end to seal the braid.

PROVING

After the dough has been shaped by hand, whether placed in a loaf tin (pan) or on a baking sheet, it will need to rise again. This process is sometimes called proving the dough.

You should avoid leaving the dough to rise for too long (called over-proving) or it may collapse in the oven or when it is slashed before baking. Equally, you need to leave it to rise sufficiently or the finished loaf will be heavy.

1 Shape the dough and place in a loaf tin (pan). The unproved dough should reach just over halfway up the sides of the tin. Leave the dough in a warm, draught-free place to rise. (An airing cupboard is ideal but ensure that the temperature remains constant.) How long this takes will vary – depending on the ambient temperature and the richness of the dough – but somewhere between 30 and 60 minutes is usual.

2 Once risen, the dough will have almost doubled in bulk. To test if the loaf is ready to bake, press it lightly with your fingertip. It should feel springy rather than firm. The indentation made by your finger should slowly fill and spring back.

SLASHING

Cutting bread dough before baking serves a useful purpose as well as adding a decorative finish. When the dough goes into the oven it has one final rise, known as "oven spring", so the cuts or slashes allow the bread to expand without tearing or cracking the sides.

The earlier you slash the dough, the wider the splits will be. Depth is important too: the deeper the slashes, the more the bread will open during baking. Most recipes suggest slashing just before glazing and baking. If the top of the loaf is to be floured, sprinkle with flour before slashing.

1 Use a sharp knife or scalpel to make a long slash, about 1 cm/½in deep along the top of a split tin or a farmhouse loaf. Plunge the blade into one end of the dough and pull it smoothly along the entire length, ensuring t

2 Use a pair of sharp-pointed scissors to slash rolls. You can create a number of quick and interesting finishes. Different finishes include: a cross, horizontal cuts around the side, and cuts from the edges almost to the centre.

GLAZES

Both machine-baked breads and hand-shaped loaves benefit from a glaze to give that final finishing touch. Glazes may be used before baking, or during the early stages of baking to give a more golden crust or to change the texture of the crust. This is particularly noticeable with hand-shaped breads but good results may also be obtained with machine-baked loaves. Glazes may also be applied after baking to give flavour and a glossy finish. Another important role for glazes is to act as an adhesive, to help any topping applied to the loaf stick to the surface of the dough.

For machine-baked breads, the glaze should either be brushed on to the loaf just before the baking cycle commences, or within 10 minutes of the start of the baking cycle. Apply the glaze quickly, so there is minimal heat loss while the bread machine lid is open. Avoid brushing the edges of the loaf with a sticky glaze as this might make the bread stick to the pan.

Glazes using egg, milk and salted water can also be brushed over freshly cooked loaves. Brush the glaze over as soon as the baking cycle finishes, then leave the bread inside the machine for 3–4 minutes, to allow the glaze to dry to a shine. Then remove the loaf from the machine and pan in the usual way. This method is useful if you want to sprinkle over a topping.

For hand-shaped loaves, you can brush with glaze before or after baking. Some recipes, such as Ginger and Raisin Whirls, suggest that you do both.

GLAZES USED BEFORE OR DURING BAKING

For a crust with an attractive glossy shine, apply a glaze before or during baking.

MILK

Brush on loaves, such as potato breads, where a softer golden crust is desired. Milk is also used for bridge rolls, buns (such as teacakes) and flatbreads where a soft crust is desirable. It can also be used on baps and soft morning rolls before dusting with flour.

OLIVE OIL

Olive oil is mainly used to brush on Mediterranean-style breads, such as focaccia and Stromboli. It adds flavour and a shiny finish; and the darker the oil the fuller the flavour, so use extra virgin olive oil for a really deep taste. Olive oil can be used before and/or after baking.

BELOW: French fougasse is brushed with olive oil just before baking.

BUTTER

Rolls and buns are brushed with melted butter before baking to add colour, while also keeping the dough soft. Bubble Corn Bread is brushed before baking to produce an enticing golden sheen on the top of the loaf. Butter is a quick and easy way to add a rich flavour to the breads glazed with it.

SALTED WATER

Mix 10ml/2 tsp salt with 30ml/2 tbsp water and brush over the dough immediately before baking. This gives a crisp baked crust with a slight sheen.

EGG WHITE

Use 1 egg white mixed with 15ml/1 tbsp water for a lighter golden, slightly shiny crust. This is often a better alternative to egg yolk for savoury breads.

EGG YOLK

Mix 1 egg yolk with 15ml/1 tbsp milk or water. This classic glaze, also known as egg wash, is used to give a very golden, shiny crust. For sweet buns, breads and yeast cakes add 15ml/1 tbsp sugar, for extra colour and flavour.

GLAZES ADDED AFTER BAKING

Some glazes are used after baking, often on sweet breads, cakes and pastries. These glazes generally give a glossy and/or sticky finish, and also help to keep the bread or cake moist. They are suited to both machine and hand-shaped breads.

BUTTER

Breads such as Italian panettone and stollen are brushed with melted butter after baking to soften the crust. Clarified butter is also sometimes used as a glaze to soften flatbreads.

HONEY, MALT, MOLASSES AND GOLDEN (LIGHT CORN) SYRUP

Liquid sweeteners can be warmed and brushed over breads, rolls, teabreads and cakes to give a soft, sweet, sticky crust. Honey is a traditional glaze and provides a lovely flavour, for example. Both malt and molasses have quite a strong flavour, so use these sparingly, matching them to compatible breads such as fruit loaves and cakes. Or you could mix them with a milder-flavoured liquid sweetener, such as golden syrup, to reduce their impact slightly.

SUGAR GLAZE

Dissolve 30–45ml/2–3 tbsp granulated sugar in the same amount of milk or water. Bring to the boil, then simmer for 1–2 minutes, until syrupy. Brush over fruit loaves or buns for a glossy sheen. For extra flavour, use rose water.

SYRUPS

Yeast cakes are often drizzled with sugar syrup, flavoured with liqueurs, spirits or lemon juice. The syrup moistens the bread, while adding a decorative and flavoursome topping at the same time.

PRESERVES

Jam or marmalade can be melted with a little liquid. Choose water, liqueur, spirits (such as rum or brandy) or fruit juice, depending on the bread to be glazed. The liquid thins the preserve and adds flavour. It can be brushed over freshly baked warm teabreads, Danish Pastries and sweet breads to a give a glossy, sticky finish. Dried fruit and nuts can then be sprinkled on top.

Select a flavoured jam to complement your bread or teacake. If in doubt, use apricot jam.

ICING (CONFECTIONERS') SUGAR GLAZE

Mix 30–45ml/2–3 tbsp icing sugar with 15ml/1 tbsp fruit juice, milk, single (light) cream (flavoured with vanilla essence [extract]) or water and drizzle or brush over warm sweet breads and cakes. You can also add a pinch of spice to the icing sugar to bring out the flavour of the loaf. Maple syrup can be mixed with the sugar for glazing nut-flavoured breads.

LEFT: The glossy top to hot cross buns is achieved by glazing after baking with a mixture of milk and sugar.

TOPPINGS

In addition to glazes, extra ingredients can be sprinkled over breads to give the finished loaf further interest. Toppings can alter the appearance, flavour and texture of the bread, so are an important part of any recipe. They also allow you to add your own individual stamp to a bread by using a topping of your own invention.

MACHINE-BAKED BREADS

A topping can be added at various stages: at the beginning of the baking cycle, about 10 minutes after baking begins, or immediately after baking while the bread is still hot. If you choose to add the topping at the beginning of baking, open the lid only for the shortest possible time, so heat loss is limited to the minimum. Before you add a topping, brush the bread with a glaze. This will ensure that the topping sticks to the loaf. Most machine breads are brushed with an egg, milk or water glaze.

If applying a topping to a bread after baking, remove the bread pan carefully from the machine and close the lid to retain the heat. Using oven gloves, quickly loosen the bread from the pan, then put it back in the pan again (this will make the

ABOVE: Fresh grapes are traditionally placed on top of the Tuscan bread, Schiacciata con Uva, to celebrate the grape harvest. The juices run freely over the loaf as it cooks.

final removal easier) then brush the loaf with the glaze and sprinkle over the chosen topping. Return the bread in the pan to the bread machine for 3–4 minutes, which allows the glaze to bake on and secure the topping. With this method, the chosen topping will not cook and brown in the same way it would were it added at the beginning of baking.

When using grain as a topping, the general rule is to match it to the grain or flour used in the bread itself; for example, a bread containing millet flakes or millet seeds is often sprinkled with millet flour.

If a flavouring has been incorporated into the dough, you may be able to top the loaf with the same ingredient, to provide a hint of what is inside. Try sprinkling a little grated Parmesan on to a cheese loaf about 10 minutes after baking begins, or, for a loaf flavoured with herbs, add an appropriate dried herb as a topping immediately after baking.

LEFT: Partybrot is brushed with egg yolk. The wholemeal rolls are sprinkled with rolled oats and the white with poppy seeds to add a delicious crunch.

FLOUR

To create a farmhouse-style finish, brush the loaf with water or milk glaze just before baking – or within 10 minutes of the start of baking – and dust lightly with flour. Use white flour, or wholemeal (whole-wheat) for a more rustic finish.

MAIZEMEAL (CORNMEAL) OR POLENTA

Use maizemeal, polenta, semolina or other speciality ingredients as a finish for breads containing these flours, brushing first with a water or milk glaze.

ROLLED OATS

These make a decorative finish for white breads and breads flavoured with oatmeal. Rolled oats are best added just before or at the very beginning of baking.

SMALL SEEDS

Seeds can be used to add flavour and texture in addition to a decorative finish. Try sesame, poppy, aniseed, caraway or cumin seeds. If adding sesame seeds immediately after baking, lightly toast until golden before adding.

LARGE SEEDS

Gently press pumpkin or sunflower seeds on to the top of a freshly glazed loaf to give an attractive finish and a bonus crunch.

PEPPER AND PAPRIKA

Freshly ground black pepper and paprika both add spiciness to savoury breads. This tasty topping can be added before, during or after baking.

SALT

Brush the top of a white loaf with water or egg glaze and sprinkle with a coarse sea salt, to give an attractive and crunchy topping. Sea salt is best applied at the beginning of baking or 10 minutes into the baking cycle.

WHEAT AND OAT BRAN FLAKES

These add both texture and fibre to bread as well as visual appeal. Sprinkle them over the top of the loaf after glazing at the beginning of baking.

ICING (CONFECTIONERS') SUGAR

Dust cooked sweet breads, teabreads or cakes with icing sugar after baking for a finished look. If wished, add 2.5ml/½tsp spice before sprinkling for added flavour.

HAND-SHAPED BREAD

All of the toppings used on machine-baked breads can also be added to breads that are hand-shaped and baked in an oven. There are several methods that can be used for adding a topping to hand-shaped rolls and breads.

SPRINKLING WITH FLOUR

If you are using flour, this should be sprinkled over the dough immediately after shaping and again before slashing and baking, to give a rustic finish. Match the flour to the type of bread being made. Unbleached strong white (bread) flour is ideal for giving soft rolls and breads a fine finish. Use maizemeal (cornmeal), ground rice or rice flour for muffins and brown and wholemeal (whole-wheat) on wholegrain breads.

GROUND RICE OR RICE FLOUR

Muffins are enhanced with a ground rice or rice flour topping.

WHOLEMEAL (WHOLE-WHEAT) FLOUR

Wholemeal flour toppings complement wholegrain dough whether made into loaves or rolls.

ABOVE: Pizza-type breads, such as this Sicilian Sfincione, feature such generous savoury toppings that the dough becomes a meal in itself.

ROLLING DOUGH IN SEEDS

Sprinkle seeds, salt or any other fine topping on a work surface, then roll the shaped but unproved dough in the chosen topping until it is evenly coated. This is ideal for coating wholegrain breads with pumpkin seeds or wheat flakes. After rolling, place the dough on the sheet for its final rising.

SESAME SEEDS

Dough sticks can be rolled in small seeds for a delicious crunchy topping.

ADDING A TOPPING AFTER A GLAZE

Some toppings are sprinkled over the bread after glazing and immediately before baking. In addition to the toppings suggested for machine-baked breads, these toppings can be used:

CANDIED FRUITS

Whole or chopped candied fruits make an attractive topping for festive breads. Add the fruits after an egg glaze. They can also be used after baking, with a jam or icing (confectioners') sugar glaze to stick the fruits to the bread.

NUTS

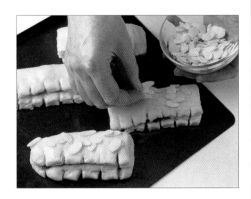

Just before baking, brush sweet or savoury breads and rolls with glaze and sprinkle with chopped or flaked (sliced) almonds, chopped cashews, and chopped or whole walnuts or pecan nuts.

SMALL SEEDS AND GRAINS

Seeds and grains, such as millet grain, black onion seeds and mustard seeds, all add texture and taste to breads. Try them as a topping for loaves and flatbreads.

VEGETABLES

Brush savoury breads and rolls with an egg glaze or olive oil and then sprinkle with finely chopped raw onion, raw (bell) peppers, sun-dried tomatoes or olives for an extremely tasty crust.

CHEESE

Grated cheeses, such as Parmesan, Cheddar or Pecorino, are best for sprinkling on to dough just before baking, resulting in a chewy, flavoursome crust.

FRESH HERBS

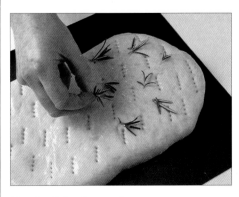

Use fresh herbs, such as rosemary, thyme, sage or basii for Italian-style flatbreads. Chopped herbs also make a good topping for rolls.

USING SUGAR AS A TOPPING

Sugar is available in many forms, so choose one for your topping carefully.

DEMERARA (RAW) SUGAR

Before baking, brush buns and cakes with butter or milk, then sprinkle with demerara sugar for a crunchy finish.

SUGAR COATING

Yeast doughs that are deep-fried, such as doughnuts, can be sprinkled or tossed in a sugar coating. Toss doughnuts in caster (superfine) sugar that has been mixed with a little ground cinnamon or freshly grated nutmeg, or flavoured using a vanilla pod (bean).

ICING (CONFECTIONERS') SUGAR

Use a fine sieve to sprinkle cooked buns and yeast cakes with a light dusting of icing (confectioners') sugar. Large cakes and breads, such as Bavarian Plum Cake or Panettone, will also benefit from a light dusting of icing sugar. If you are serving a bread or cake warm, dust with icing sugar when ready to serve to prevent the topping from soaking into the bread.

FROM BASIC BREADS TO SPECIALITY GRAINS

This selection of recipes includes classic flours from around the world, producing loaves with a variety of textures and flavours. Gluten is an essential part of the structure of bread, to ensure an open, light crumb and texture. Most grains other than wheat have little or no gluten, so millet, barley and rye have been blended with wheat flours to provide rich, nutty flavoured loaves which can be successfully baked in your bread machine.

SMALL
210ml/7½fl oz/scant 1 cup water
22ml/1½ tbsp sunflower oil
375g/13oz/3¼ cups unbleached strong
white (bread) flour
15ml/1 tbsp skimmed milk powder
(non fat dry milk)
7.5ml/1½ tsp salt
15ml/1 tbsp granulated sugar
5ml/1 tsp easy-blend (rapid-rise)
dried yeast

MEDIUM
315ml/11fl oz/1⅓ cups water
30ml/2 tbsp sunflower oil
500g/1lb 2oz/4½ cups unbleached
strong white flour
22ml/1½ tbsp skimmed milk powder
7.5ml/1½ tsp salt
22ml/1½ tbsp granulated sugar
7.5ml/1½ tsp easy-blend dried yeast

LARGE
420ml/15fl oz/scant 2 cups water
45ml/3 tbsp sunflower oil
675g/1½lb/6 cups unbleached strong
white flour
30ml/2 tbsp skimmed milk powder
10ml/2 tsp salt
30ml/2 tbsp granulated sugar
10ml/2 tsp easy-blend dried yeast

MAKES 1 LOAF

1 Pour the water and the sunflower oil into the bread machine pan. However, if the instructions for your particular machine specify that the yeast is to be placed in the pan first, then reverse the order in which you add the liquid and dry ingredients.

RAPID WHITE BREAD

A delicious basic white loaf which can be cooked on the fastest setting. It is the ideal bread if you are in a hurry.

2 Sprinkle in the flour, covering the water. Add the milk powder. Place the salt and sugar in separate corners of the bread pan. Make a shallow indent in the centre of the flour (but not down as far as the liquid) and add the yeast.

3 Set the bread machine to the rapid/quick setting, medium crust. Press Start.

4 Remove the bread at the end of the baking cycle and turn out on to a wire rack to cool.

COOK'S TIP
On the quick setting the yeast has less time to work, and breads may not rise so high as those cooked on the basic/normal setting.
In cold weather it may be necessary to use lukewarm water, to help speed up the action of the yeast.

MILK LOAF

Adding milk results in a soft, velvety grained loaf with a beautifully browned crust. Milk also improves the keeping quality of the bread.

SMALL
180ml/6½fl oz/generous ¾ cup milk
50ml/2fl oz/¼ cup water
*375g/13oz/3¼ cups unbleached strong
white (bread) flour*
7.5ml/1½ tsp salt
10ml/2 tsp granulated sugar
20g/¾oz/1½ tbsp butter
*2.5ml/½ tsp easy-blend (rapid-rise)
dried yeast*

MEDIUM
200ml/7fl oz/⅞ cup milk
100ml/3½fl oz/7 tbsp water
*450g/1lb/4 cups unbleached strong
white flour*
7.5ml/1½ tsp salt
10ml/2 tsp granulated sugar
25g/1oz/2 tbsp butter
5ml/1 tsp easy-blend dried yeast

LARGE
280ml/10fl oz/1¼ cups milk
130ml/4½fl oz/½ cup + 1 tbsp water
*675g/1½lb/6 cups unbleached strong
white flour*
10ml/2 tsp salt
15ml/1 tbsp granulated sugar
25g/1oz/2 tbsp butter
7.5ml/1½ tsp easy-blend dried yeast

MAKES 1 LOAF

COOK'S TIP

Ensure the milk used for this bread
is at room temperature or it will
retard the action of the yeast and the
bread will not rise properly. Remove
it from the refrigerator 30 minutes
before using. You can use either
full-cream or semi-skimmed (low fat)
milk for this recipe.

1 Pour the milk and water into the bread machine pan. If the instructions for your machine specify that the yeast is to be placed in the pan first, reverse the order in which you add the liquid and dry ingredients.

2 Sprinkle in the flour, making sure that it covers the water. Add the salt, sugar and butter in separate corners of the bread pan. Make a small indent in the centre of the flour, but not down as far as the liquid, and add the yeast.

3 Set the bread machine to the basic/ normal setting, medium crust, then press Start.

4 Remove the bread at the end of the baking cycle and turn out on to a wire rack to cool.

SMALL
210ml/7½fl oz/scant 1 cup water
375g/13oz/3¼ cups unbleached strong
white (bread) flour
7.5ml/1½ tsp salt
15ml/1 tbsp granulated sugar
25g/1oz/2 tbsp butter
5ml/1 tsp easy-blend (rapid-rise)
dried yeast
unbleached strong white (bread)
flour, for dusting

MEDIUM
320ml/11¼fl oz/generous
1⅓ cups water
500g/1lb 2oz/4½ cups unbleached
strong white flour
7.5ml/1½ tsp salt
15ml/1 tbsp granulated sugar
25g/1oz/2 tbsp butter
5ml/1 tsp easy-blend dried yeast
unbleached strong white (bread)
flour, for dusting

LARGE
420ml/15fl oz/generous 1¾ cups water
675g/1½lb/6 cups unbleached strong
white flour
10ml/2 tsp salt
22ml/1½ tbsp granulated sugar
40g/1½oz/3 tbsp butter
7.5ml/1½ tsp easy-blend dried yeast
unbleached strong white flour;
for dusting

MAKES 1 LOAF

WHITE BREAD

This is a simple all-purpose white bread recipe, which makes the perfect basis for experimenting. Try using different brands of flours and be prepared to make minor alterations to quantities if necessary, to find the optimum recipe for your machine.

1 Pour the water into the bread machine pan. However, if the instructions for your machine specify that the yeast is to be placed in the pan first, reverse the order in which you add the liquid and dry ingredients.

2 Sprinkle in the flour, making sure that it covers the water. Add the salt, sugar and butter in separate corners of the bread pan. Make a small indent in the centre of the flour, but not down as far as the liquid, and add the yeast.

COOK'S TIP
To give the crust a richer golden appearance, add skimmed milk powder (non fat dry milk) to the flour. For a small loaf, use 15ml/1 tbsp; for a medium loaf 22ml/1½ tbsp and for a large loaf 30ml/2 tbsp.

3 Set the bread machine to the basic/normal setting, medium crust and then press Start.

4 Remove the bread at the end of the baking cycle and turn out on to a wire rack to cool.

ANADAMA BREAD

—

*This traditional New England bread is made with a mixture of white and
wholemeal flours and polenta, which is a coarse maizemeal.
The molasses sweetens the bread and gives it a rich colour.*

SMALL
*200ml/7fl oz/⅞ cup water
45ml/3 tbsp molasses
5ml/1 tsp lemon juice
275g/10oz/2½ cups unbleached strong
white (bread) flour
65g/2½oz/generous ½ cup strong
wholemeal (whole-wheat) flour
40g/1½oz/⅓ cup polenta
7.5ml/1½ tsp salt
25g/1oz/2 tbsp butter
5ml/1 tsp easy-blend (rapid-rise)
dried yeast*

MEDIUM
*240ml/8½fl oz/generous 1 cup water
60ml/4 tbsp molasses
5ml/1 tsp lemon juice
360g/12½oz/generous 3 cups
unbleached strong white flour
75g/3oz/¾ cup strong wholemeal flour
65g/2½oz/generous ½ cup polenta
10ml/2 tsp salt
40g/1½oz/3 tbsp butter
5ml/1 tsp easy-blend dried yeast*

LARGE
*280ml/10fl oz/1¼ cups water
90ml/5 tbsp molasses
10ml/2 tsp lemon juice
500g/1lb 2oz/4¼ cups unbleached
strong white flour
90g/generous 3oz/scant 1 cup strong
wholemeal flour
75g/3oz/¾ cup polenta
12.5ml/2½ tsp salt
50g/2oz/¼ cup butter
10ml/2 tsp easy-blend dried yeast*

MAKES 1 LOAF

COOK'S TIP
Check the moistness of the dough
after a couple of minutes' kneading. If
rather dry, cautiously add a little water.

1 Pour the water, molasses and lemon juice into the bread machine pan. If the instructions for your machine specify that the yeast is to be placed in the pan first, reverse the order in which you add the liquid and dry ingredients.

2 Sprinkle in both types of flour, then the polenta, so that the water is completely covered. Add the salt and butter in separate corners of the bread pan. Make a small indent in the centre of the flour and add the yeast.

3 Set the bread machine to the basic/normal setting, medium crust. Press Start.

4 Remove the bread at the end of the baking cycle and turn out on to a wire rack to cool.

SMALL
230ml/8fl oz/1 cup buttermilk
30ml/2 tbsp water
15ml/1 tbsp clear honey
15ml/1 tbsp sunflower oil
*250g/9oz/2¼ cups unbleached strong
white (bread) flour*
*125g/4½oz/generous 1 cup strong
wholemeal (whole-wheat) flour*
7.5ml/1½ tsp salt
*5ml/1 tsp easy-blend (rapid-rise)
dried yeast*

MEDIUM
285ml/10fl oz/1¼ cups buttermilk
65ml/4½ tbsp water
22ml/1½ tbsp clear honey
22ml/1½ tbsp sunflower oil
*350g/12oz/3 cups unbleached strong
white (bread) flour*
*150g/5½oz/1⅓ cup strong
wholemeal flour*
7.5ml/1½ tsp salt
*7.5ml/1½ tsp easy-blend
dried yeast*

LARGE
*370ml/13fl oz/scant 1⅝ cups
buttermilk*
80ml/5½ tbsp water
30ml/2 tbsp clear honey
30ml/2 tbsp sunflower oil
*475g/1lb 1oz/4¼ cups unbleached
strong white (bread) flour*
*200g/7oz/1¾ cups strong
wholemeal flour*
10ml/2 tsp salt
10ml/2 tsp easy-blend dried yeast

MAKES 1 LOAF

COOK'S TIP
Buttermilk is a by-product of butter
making, and is the liquid left after the
fat has been made into butter. It is
pasteurized and mixed with a special
culture which causes it to ferment,
resulting in the characteristic slightly
sour flavour. If you run short of
buttermilk, using a low-fat natural
(plain) yogurt and 5–10ml/1–2 tsp
lemon juice is an alternative.

BUTTERMILK BREAD

*Buttermilk adds a pleasant, slightly sour note to the flavour of this bread. It
also gives the bread a good light texture and a golden brown crust. Buttermilk
bread tastes especially delicious when toasted and simply spread with a little
good-quality butter.*

1 Pour the buttermilk, water, honey and
oil into the bread machine pan. If your
instructions specify that the yeast is to
be placed in the pan first, reverse the
order of the liquid and dry ingredients.

2 Sprinkle over both the white and
wholemeal flours, making sure that the
water is completely covered. Add the
salt in one corner of the bread pan.
Make a small indent in the centre of the
flour, but not down as far as the liquid,
and add the yeast.

3 Set the bread machine to the basic/
normal setting, medium crust and then
press Start.

4 Remove the bread from the pan at the
end of the baking cycle and turn out on
to a wire rack to cool.

GRANARY BREAD

---

*Granary, or multi-grain, flour – like Malthouse flour – is a blend, and
contains malted wheat grain which gives a crunchy texture to this loaf.*

1 Add the water to the bread machine
pan. If the instructions for your machine
specify that the yeast is to be placed in
the pan first, simply reverse the order
in which you add the liquid and dry
ingredients to the pan.

2 Sprinkle in the flour, making sure that
it covers the water. Add the salt, sugar
and butter in separate corners of the
bread pan. Make a small indent in the
centre of the flour, but not down as far
as the liquid, and add the yeast.

3 Set the bread machine to the whole
wheat or multi-grain setting, medium
crust. Press Start.

4 Remove the bread at the end of the
baking cycle and turn out on to a wire
rack to cool.

COOK'S TIP
This bread tastes just as good if you
use Malthouse bread flour instead of
Granary (multi-grain) flour.

SMALL
240ml/8½fl oz/generous 1 cup water
375g/13oz/3¼ cups Granary
(multi-grain) flour
5ml/1 tsp salt
10ml/2 tsp granulated sugar
20g/¾oz/1½ tbsp butter
2.5ml/½tsp easy-blend (rapid-rise)
dried yeast

MEDIUM
350ml/12fl oz/1½ cups water
500g/1lb 2oz/4½ cups Granary flour
7.5ml/1½ tsp salt
15ml/1 tbsp granulated sugar
25g/1oz/2 tbsp butter
7.5ml/1½ tsp easy-blend dried yeast

LARGE
400ml/14fl oz/generous 1⅔ cups water
675g/1½lb/6 cups Granary flour
10ml/2 tsp salt
15ml/1 tbsp granulated sugar
25g/1oz/2 tbsp butter
7.5ml/1½ tsp easy-blend dried yeast

MAKES 1 LOAF

SMALL
230ml/8fl oz/1 cup water
30ml/2 tbsp sunflower oil
30ml/2 tbsp molasses
115g/4oz/1 cup rye flour
50g/2oz/½ cup strong wholemeal
(whole-wheat bread) flour
175g/6oz/1½ cups unbleached strong
white (bread) flour
25g/1oz/2 tbsp oat bran
50g/2oz/½ cup dried breadcrumbs
15ml/1 tbsp (unsweetened) cocoa powder
30ml/2 tbsp instant coffee granules
7.5ml/1½ tsp caraway seeds
5ml/1 tsp salt
5ml/1 tsp easy-blend (rapid-rise)
dried yeast

MEDIUM
360ml/12½fl oz/generous 1½ cups water
30ml/2 tbsp sunflower oil
40ml/2½ tbsp molasses
140g/5oz/1¼ cups rye flour
85g/3oz/¾ cup strong wholemeal flour
250g/9oz/2¼ cups unbleached strong
white flour
40g/1½oz/3 tbsp oat bran
75g/3oz/¾ cup dried breadcrumbs
22ml/1½ tbsp cocoa powder
40ml/2½ tbsp instant coffee granules
7.5ml/1½ tsp caraway seeds
7.5ml/1½ tsp salt
7.5ml/1½ tsp easy-blend dried yeast

LARGE
430ml/15fl oz/generous 1⅔ cups water
45ml/3 tbsp sunflower oil
45ml/3 tbsp molasses
200g/7oz/1¾ cups rye flour
100g/3½oz/scant 1 cup strong
wholemeal flour
300g/10½oz/generous 2½ cups
unbleached strong white flour
50g/2oz/4 tbsp oat bran
100g/3½oz/scant 1 cup dried
breadcrumbs
30ml/2 tbsp cocoa powder
45ml/3 tbsp instant coffee granules
10ml/2 tsp caraway seeds
10ml/2 tsp salt
10ml/2 tsp easy-blend dried yeast

MAKES 1 LOAF

RUSSIAN BLACK BREAD

European rye breads often include cocoa and coffee to add colour to this dark traditionally dense, chewy bread. Slice it thinly, serve it with cold meats or pâtés or use it as the basis of an open sandwich.

1 Pour the water, sunflower oil and molasses into the bread machine pan. If the instructions for your machine specify that the yeast is to be placed in the bread pan first, then simply reverse the order in which you add the liquid and dry ingredients.

2 Sprinkle over the rye, wholemeal and white flours, then the oat bran and breadcrumbs, making sure that the water is completely covered. Add the cocoa powder, coffee granules, caraway seeds and salt. Make a small indent in the centre of the flour, but not down as far as the liquid, and add the easy-blend dried yeast.

3 Set the bread machine to the whole wheat setting, medium crust and then press Start.

4 Remove the bread at the end of the baking cycle and turn out on to a wire rack to cool.

MULTIGRAIN BREAD

This healthy, mixed grain bread owes its wonderfully rich flavour to honey and malt extract.

2 Sprinkle in all four types of flour, making sure that the liquid is completely covered. Add the jumbo oats and skimmed milk powder.

3 Place the salt and butter in separate corners of the bread machine pan. Make a small indent in the centre of the flour, but not down as far as the liquid, and add the yeast.

1 Add the water, honey and malt extract to the pan. If your machine's instructions specify that the yeast is to be placed in the pan first, reverse the order in which you add the liquid and dry ingredients.

4 Set the bread machine to the whole wheat setting, medium crust. Press Start. Remove the bread at the end of the baking cycle and turn out on to a wire rack to cool.

SMALL
230ml/8fl oz/1 cup water
15ml/1 tbsp clear honey
7.5ml/1½ tsp malt extract
115g/4oz/1 cup Granary
(multi-grain) flour
50g/2oz/½ cup rye flour
75g/3oz/¾ cup unbleached strong
white (bread) flour
140g/5oz/1¼ cups strong wholemeal
(whole-wheat bread) flour
15ml/1 tbsp jumbo oats
15ml/1 tbsp skimmed milk powder
(non fat dry milk)
5ml/1 tsp salt
20g/¾oz/1½ tbsp butter
4ml/¾ tsp easy-blend (rapid-rise)
dried yeast

MEDIUM
300ml/10½fl oz/scant 1⅓ cups water
30ml/2 tbsp clear honey
15ml/1 tbsp malt extract
150g/5½oz/1⅓ cups Granary flour
75g/3oz/¾ cup rye flour
75g/3oz/¾ cup unbleached strong
white (bread) flour
200g/7oz/1¾ cups strong
wholemeal flour
30ml/2 tbsp jumbo oats
30ml/2 tbsp skimmed milk powder
7.5ml/1½ tsp salt
25g/1oz/2 tbsp butter
5ml/1 tsp easy-blend dried yeast

LARGE
375ml/13fl oz/scant 1⅔ cups water
30ml/2 tbsp clear honey
22ml/1½ tbsp malt extract
200g/7oz/1¾ cups Granary flour
115g/4oz/1 cup rye flour
115g/4oz/1 cup unbleached strong
white (bread) flour
225g/8oz/2 cups strong
wholemeal flour
45ml/3 tbsp jumbo oats
45ml/3 tbsp skimmed milk powder
10ml/2 tsp salt
40g/1½ oz/3 tbsp butter
7.5ml/1½ tsp easy-blend dried yeast

MAKES 1 LOAF

280ml/10fl oz/1¼ cups water
30ml/2 tbsp extra virgin olive oil
*400g/14oz/3½ cups unbleached strong
white (bread) flour*
50g/2oz/½ cup millet flour
*50g/2oz/½ cup strong wholemeal
(whole-wheat bread) flour*
15ml/1 tbsp granulated sugar
10ml/2 tsp salt
*5ml/1 tsp easy-blend (rapid-rise)
dried yeast*
30ml/2 tbsp pumpkin seeds
30ml/2 tbsp sunflower seeds
22ml/1½ tbsp linseeds
*22ml/1½ tbsp sesame seeds,
lightly toasted*

FOR THE TOPPING
15ml/1 tbsp milk
30ml/2 tbsp golden linseeds

MAKES 1 LOAF

1 Pour the water and oil into the bread
pan. Add the dry ingredients first, if
your bread machine specifies this.

2 Sprinkle in all three types of flour,
making sure that the water is covered.
Add the sugar and salt in separate
corners of the bread pan.

3 Make a shallow indent in the centre of
the flour and add the yeast. Set the
bread machine to the dough setting; use
basic raisin dough setting (if available).
Press Start. Add the seeds when the
machine beeps to add extra ingredients
or during the last 5 minutes of kneading.

4 When the dough cycle has finished,
place the dough on a lightly floured
surface and knock back (punch down).

FOUR SEED BREAD

*This light wholemeal and millet bread has added bite, thanks to a variety of
tasty seeds, all readily available from your local health-food store.*

5 Lightly oil a baking sheet. Shape the
dough into a round flat loaf. Make a hole
in the centre with your finger. Gradually
enlarge the cavity, turning the dough,
until you have a ring. Place the ring on
the baking sheet. Cover it with lightly
oiled clear film (plastic wrap) and leave
it in a warm place for 30–45 minutes, or
until the dough has doubled in size.

6 Meanwhile, preheat the oven to 200°C/
400°F/Gas 6. Brush the top of the bread
with milk and sprinkle it with the golden
linseeds. Make slashes around the loaf,
radiating outwards.

7 Bake for 30–35 minutes, or until
golden and hollow-sounding. Turn out
on to a wire rack to cool.

HAZELNUT AND FIG BREAD

—

This healthy, high-fibre bread is flavoured with figs and hazelnuts.

SMALL
230ml/8fl oz/1 cup water
5ml/1 tsp lemon juice
280g/10oz/2½ cups unbleached strong
white (bread) flour
75g/3oz/¾ cup strong brown (bread)
flour
45ml/3 tbsp toasted wheatgerm
15ml/1 tbsp skimmed milk powder
(non fat dry milk)
5ml/1 tsp salt
10ml/2 tsp granulated sugar
20g/¾oz/1½ tbsp butter
5ml/1 tsp easy-blend (rapid-rise)
dried yeast
25g/1oz/3 tbsp skinned hazelnuts,
roasted and chopped
25g/1oz/3 tbsp ready-to-eat dried figs

MEDIUM
280ml/10fl oz/1¼ cups water
7.5ml/1½ tsp lemon juice
350g/12oz/3 cups unbleached strong
white flour
100g/3½oz/scant 1 cup strong
brown flour
60ml/4 tbsp toasted wheatgerm
30ml/2 tbsp skimmed milk powder
7.5ml/1½ tsp salt
15ml/1 tbsp granulated sugar
25g/1oz/2 tbsp butter
7.5ml/1½ tsp easy-blend dried yeast
40g/1½oz/¼ cup ready-to-eat
dried figs
40g/1½oz/⅓ cup skinned hazelnuts,
roasted and chopped

1 Pour the water and the lemon juice into the bread machine pan. If the instructions for your machine specify that the yeast is to be placed in the pan first, reverse the order in which you add the liquid and dry ingredients.

2 Sprinkle in the flours, then the wheatgerm, covering the water. Add the milk powder. Add the salt, sugar and butter in separate corners. Make an indent in the flour; add the yeast.

3 Set the bread machine to the basic/ normal setting; use raisin setting (if available), medium crust. Press Start. Coarsely chop the dried figs. Add the hazelnuts and the figs to the bread pan when the machine beeps or after the first kneading has finished.

4 Remove the Bread at the end of the baking cycle and turn out on to a wire rack to cool.

LARGE
450ml/16fl oz/scant 2 cups water
10ml/2 tsp lemon juice
500g/1lb 2oz/4½ cups unbleached
strong white flour
115g/4oz/1 cup strong brown flour
75ml/5 tbsp toasted wheatgerm
45ml/3 tbsp skimmed milk powder
10ml/2 tsp salt
20ml/4 tsp granulated sugar
40g/1½oz/3 tbsp butter
7.5ml/1½ tsp easy-blend dried yeast
50g/2oz/⅓ cup ready-to-eat dried figs
50g/2oz/½ cup skinned hazelnuts,
roasted and chopped

MAKES 1 LOAF

TOASTED MILLET AND RYE BREAD

300ml/10½fl oz/1¼ cups water
50g/2oz/½ cup rye flour
450g/1lb/4 cups unbleached strong
white (bread) flour
25g/1oz/¼ cup millet flakes
15ml/1 tbsp light muscovado
(molasses) sugar
5ml/1 tsp salt
25g/1oz/2 tbsp butter
5ml/1 tsp easy-blend (rapid-rise)
dried yeast
50g/2oz/⅓ cup millet seeds
millet flour, for dusting

MAKES 1 LOAF

*The dough for this delectable loaf is made in the bread machine, but it is
shaped by hand before being baked in the oven.*

1 Pour the water into the bread pan. If the instructions for your bread machine specify that the yeast is to be placed in the pan first, reverse the order in which you add the liquid and dry ingredients.

2 Sprinkle in both types of flour, then add the millet flakes, making sure that the water is completely covered. Add the sugar, salt and butter, placing them in separate corners. Make an indent in the centre of the flour, but not down as far as the liquid, and add the yeast.

3 Set the bread machine to the dough setting; use basic raisin dough setting (if available). Press Start. Add the millet seeds when the machine beeps or during the last 5 minutes of kneading. Lightly flour a baking sheet.

4 When the dough cycle has finished, knock back (punch down) the dough gently on a lightly floured surface.

5 Shape the dough into a rectangle. Roll it up lengthways, then shape it into a thick baton with square ends. Place it on the baking sheet, making sure that the seam is underneath. Cover it with lightly oiled clear film (plastic wrap) and leave in a warm place for 30–45 minutes, or until almost doubled in size.

6 Remove the clear film and dust the top of the loaf with the millet flour. Using a sharp knife, make slanting cuts in alternate directions along the top of the loaf. Leave it to stand for about 10 minutes. Meanwhile, preheat the oven to 220°C/425°F/Gas 7.

7 Bake the loaf for 25–30 minutes, or until golden and hollow-sounding. Turn out on to a wire rack to cool.

LIGHT RYE AND CARAWAY BREAD

*Rye flour adds a distinctive slightly sour flavour to bread. Rye breads can be
dense, so the flour is usually mixed with wheat flour to lighten the texture.*

1 Add the water, lemon juice and oil to
the bread pan. If your instructions
specify that the yeast is to be placed in
the pan first, reverse the order in which
you add the liquid and dry ingredients.

2 Sprinkle in the rye flour and the white
bread flour, making sure they cover the
water. Add the skimmed milk powder
and caraway seeds. Add the salt and
sugar in separate corners of the bread
pan. Make a small indent in the centre
of the flour, but not down as far as the
liquid, and add the yeast.

3 Set the bread machine to the basic/
normal setting, medium crust and then
press Start.

4 Remove the bread from the pan at the
end of the cycle and transfer to a wire
rack to cool.

SMALL

210ml/7½fl oz/scant 1 cup water

5ml/1 tsp lemon juice

15ml/1 tbsp sunflower oil

85g/3oz/¾ cup rye flour

*285g/10oz/2½ cups unbleached strong
white (bread) flour*

*15ml/1 tbsp skimmed milk powder
(non fat dry milk)*

5ml/1 tsp caraway seeds

5ml/1 tsp salt

*10ml/2 tsp light brown muscovado
(molasses) sugar*

*3.5ml/¾ tsp easy-blend (rapid-rise)
dried yeast*

MEDIUM

300ml/10½fl oz/1¼ cups water

10ml/2 tsp lemon juice

22ml/1½ tbsp sunflower oil

125g/4½oz/generous 1 cup rye flour

*375g/13oz/3¼ cups unbleached
strong white flour*

22ml/1½ tbsp skimmed milk powder

7.5ml/1½ tsp caraway seeds

7.5ml/1½ tsp salt

*15ml/1 tbsp light brown
muscovado sugar*

5ml/1 tsp easy-blend dried yeast

LARGE

370ml/13fl oz/scant 1⅝ cups water

10ml/2 tsp lemon juice

30ml/2 tbsp sunflower oil

*175g/generous 6oz/generous 1½ cups
rye flour*

*500g/1lb 2oz/4½ cups unbleached
strong white flour*

30ml/2 tbsp skimmed milk powder

10ml/2 tsp caraway seeds

10ml/2 tsp salt

*20ml/4 tsp light brown
muscovado sugar*

7.5ml/1½ tsp easy-blend dried yeast

MAKES 1 LOAF

For the Milk Rolls
145ml/5fl oz/scant ⅔ cup milk
225g/8oz/2 cups unbleached strong
white (bread) flour
7.5ml/1½ tsp granulated sugar
5ml/1 tsp salt
15g/½oz/1 tbsp butter
2.5ml/½ tsp easy-blend (rapid-rise)
dried yeast

For the Wholemeal
(whole-wheat) Rolls
175ml/6fl oz/¾ cup water
175g/6oz/1½ cups strong wholemeal
(whole-wheat bread) flour
75g/3oz/¾ cup unbleached
strong white flour
7.5ml/1½ tsp granulated sugar
5ml/1 tsp salt
25g/1oz/2 tbsp butter
2.5ml/½ tsp easy-blend (rapid-rise)
dried yeast

For the Topping
1 egg yolk 15ml/1 tbsp rolled oats or
cracked wheat
15ml/1 tbsp poppy seeds

Makes 19 Rolls

1 Pour the milk for making the milk
rolls into the bread machine pan.
However, if the instructions for your
bread machine specify that the yeast is
to be placed in the pan first, simply
reverse the order in which you add the
wet and dry ingredients.

2 Sprinkle in the strong white flour,
making sure that it covers the milk
completely. Add the sugar, salt and
butter, placing them in separate corners
of the bread pan.

3 Make a small indent in the centre of
the flour, but not down as far as the
liquid underneath, and add the easy-
blend dried yeast.

4 Set the bread machine to the dough
setting; use basic dough setting (if
available). Press Start.

PARTYBROT

These traditional Swiss-German rolls are baked as one, in a round tin.
As the name suggests, partybrot is perfect for entertaining.

5 Lightly oil a 25cm/10in springform or
loose-based cake tin (pan), and a large
mixing bowl. When the dough cycle has
finished, remove the dough from the
machine and place it in the mixing bowl.

6 Cover the dough with oiled clear film
(plastic wrap) and put it in the
refrigerator. To make the wholemeal
dough follow the instructions for the
milk roll dough, but using water.

7 Remove the milk roll dough from the
refrigerator 20 minutes before the end
of the wholemeal dough cycle. Remove
the wholemeal dough when ready and
place on a lightly floured surface. Knock
back (punch down) gently. Do the same
with the milk roll dough.

8 Divide the milk roll dough into nine
pieces and the wholemeal dough into 10.
Shape each piece of dough into a small
round ball.

9 Place 12 balls, equally spaced, around
the outer edge of the prepared cake tin,
alternating milk dough with wholemeal.

10 Add an inner circle with six more
balls and place the remaining ball of
wholemeal dough in the centre.

11 Cover the tin with lightly oiled clear
film and leave the rolls to rise in a warm
place for 30–45 minutes, or until they
have doubled in size. Meanwhile,
preheat the oven to 200°C/400°F/Gas 6.

12 Mix the egg yolk with 15ml/1 tbsp
cold water and brush the wholemeal
rolls. Sprinkle with rolled oats or
cracked wheat. Glaze the white rolls and
sprinkle with poppy seeds. Bake for
35–40 minutes, until the partybrot is
golden. Leave for 5 minutes to cool in
the tin, then turn out on to a wire rack.

FLATBREADS AND PIZZAS

Flatbreads are fun to bake and make delicious meal accompaniments. Naan, often flavoured with coriander or black onion seeds, is typical of Indian flatbread, whilst Lavash, Pitta and Pide are traditional Middle Eastern specialities. Italy is famous for Focaccia, pizzas and Calzone, while the French version of pizza is the Pissaladière. All of these breads can be made in your machine using the "dough only" setting and then hand-shaped and oven-baked.

GARLIC AND CORIANDER NAAN

100ml/3½ fl oz/7 tbsp water
60ml/4 tbsp natural (plain) yogurt
*280g/10oz/2½ cups unbleached strong
white (bread) flour*
1 garlic clove, finely chopped
5ml/1 tsp black onion seeds
5ml/1 tsp ground coriander
5ml/1 tsp salt
10ml/2 tsp clear honey
*15ml/1 tbsp melted ghee or butter,
plus extra for brushing*
*5ml/1 tsp easy-blend (rapid-rise)
dried yeast*
*15ml/1 tbsp chopped fresh
coriander (cilantro)*

MAKES 3 FLATBREADS

VARIATION
For a basic naan omit the coriander, garlic and black onion seeds. Include a little ground black pepper or chilli powder for a slightly piquant note.

Indian restaurants the world over have introduced us to several differently flavoured examples of this leavened flatbread, and this version is particularly tasty and will become a great favourite. The bread is traditionally made in a tandoor oven, but this method has been developed to give almost identical results.

1 Pour the water and natural yogurt into the bread machine pan. If the instructions for your bread machine specify that the easy-blend dried yeast is to be placed in the pan first, then simply reverse the order in which you add the liquid and dry ingredients.

2 Sprinkle in the flour, making sure that it covers the liquid completely. Add the garlic, black onion seeds and ground coriander. Add the salt, honey and 15ml/1 tbsp melted ghee or butter in separate corners of the bread pan. Make a small indent in the centre of the flour, but not down as far as the liquid, and add the easy-blend dried yeast.

3 Set the bread machine to the dough setting; use basic or pizza dough setting (if available). Press Start.

4 When the dough cycle has finished, preheat the oven to its highest setting. Place three baking sheets in the oven to heat. Remove the dough from the breadmaking machine and place it on a lightly floured surface.

5 Knock back (punch down) the dough gently and then knead in the chopped fresh coriander. Divide the dough into three equal pieces.

6 Shape each piece into a ball and cover two of the pieces with oiled clear film (plastic wrap). Roll out the remaining piece of dough into a large teardrop shape, making it about 5–8mm/¼–⅓in thick. Cover with oiled clear film while you roll out the remaining two pieces of dough to make two more naan.

7 Preheat the grill (broiler) to its highest setting. Place the naan on the preheated baking sheets and then bake them for 4–5 minutes, until puffed up. Remove the baking sheets from the oven and place them under the hot grill for a few seconds, until the naan start to brown and blister.

8 Brush the naan with melted ghee or butter and serve warm.

CARTA DI MUSICA

This crunchy, crisp bread looks like sheets of music manuscript paper, which is how it came by its name. It originated in Sardinia and can be found throughout southern Italy, where it is eaten not only as a bread, but as a substitute for pasta in lasagne. It also makes a good pizza base.

280ml/10fl oz/1¼ cups water
450g/1lb/4 cups unbleached strong white (bread) flour
7.5ml/1½ tsp salt
5ml/1 tsp granulated sugar
5ml/1 tsp easy-blend (rapid-rise) dried yeast

MAKES 8 FLATBREADS

COOK'S TIP
Cutting the partially cooked breads in half is quite tricky. You may find it easier to divide the dough into six or eight pieces, and roll these as thinly as possible before baking. The cutting stage can then be avoided.

1 Pour the water into the bread machine pan. If the instructions specify that the yeast should be placed in the pan first, simply reverse the order in which you add the liquid and dry ingredients to the pan.

2 Sprinkle in the strong white flour, making sure that it covers the water. Add the salt in one corner of the bread pan and the sugar in another corner. Make a small indent in the centre of the flour, but not down as far as the liquid, and add the easy-blend dried yeast.

3 Set the bread machine to the dough setting; use basic dough setting (if available). Press Start.

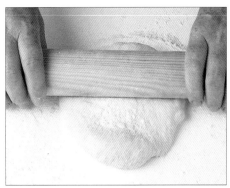

4 When the dough cycle has finished, remove the dough from the machine and place it on a lightly floured surface. Knock back (punch down) gently and divide it into four equal pieces. Shape each piece of dough into a ball, then roll a piece out until about 3mm/⅛in thick.

5 Now roll out the other three pieces. If the dough starts to tear, cover it with oiled clear film and leave it to rest for 2–3 minutes.

6 When all the dough has been rolled out, cover with oiled clear film and leave to rest on the floured surface for 10–15 minutes. Preheat the oven to 230°C/450°F/Gas 8. Place two baking sheets in the oven to heat.

7 Keeping the other dough rounds covered, place one round on each baking sheet. Bake for 5 minutes, or until puffed up.

8 Remove from the oven and cut each round in half horizontally to make two thinner breads. Place these cut-side up on the baking sheets, return them to the oven and bake for 5–8 minutes more, until crisp. Turn out on to a wire rack and cook the remaining breads.

LAVASH

250ml/generous 8½fl oz/generous
1 cup water
45ml/3 tbsp natural (plain) yogurt
350g/12oz/3 cups unbleached strong
white (bread) flour
115g/4oz/1 cup strong wholemeal
(whole-wheat) flour
5ml/1 tsp salt
5ml/1 tsp easy-blend (rapid-rise)
dried yeast

FOR THE TOPPING
30ml/2 tbsp milk
30ml/2 tbsp millet seeds

MAKES 10 FLATBREADS

VARIATION
Instead of making individual lavash
you could divide the dough into five
or six pieces and make large lavash.
Serve these on a platter in the centre
of the table and invite guests to break
off pieces as required.

*These Middle Eastern flatbreads puff up slightly during cooking, to make a
bread which is crispy, but not as dry and crisp as a cracker. Serve warm
straight from the oven or cold, with a little butter, if you like.*

1 Pour the water and yogurt into the bread machine pan. If the instructions for your machine specify that the yeast is to be placed in the pan first, reverse the order in which you add the liquid and dry ingredients.

2 Sprinkle in both types of flour, making sure that the liquid is completely covered. Add the salt in one corner of the bread pan. Make an indent in the centre of the flour and add the yeast.

3 Set the bread machine to the dough setting; use basic or pizza dough setting (if available). Press Start.

4 When the dough cycle has finished, place the dough on a lightly floured surface. Knock back (punch down) gently and divide it into 10 equal pieces.

5 Shape each piece into a ball, then flatten into a disc with your hand. Cover with oiled clear film (plastic wrap) and leave to rest for 5 minutes. Preheat the oven to 230°C/450°F/Gas 8. Place three or four baking sheets in the oven.

6 Roll each ball of dough out very thinly, then stretch it over the backs of your hands, to make the lavash. If the dough starts to tear, leave it to rest for a few minutes after rolling. Stack the lavash between layers of oiled clear film and cover to keep moist.

7 Place as many lavash as will fit comfortably on each baking sheet, brush with milk and sprinkle with millet seeds. Bake for 5–8 minutes, or until puffed and starting to brown. Transfer to a wire rack and cook the remaining lavash.

PITTA BREADS

210ml/7½fl oz/scant 1 cup water
15ml/1 tbsp olive oil
350g/12oz/3 cups unbleached strong
white (bread) flour
7.5ml/1½ tsp salt
5ml/1 tsp granulated sugar
5ml/1 tsp easy-blend (rapid-rise)
dried yeast

MAKES 6–10 FLATBREADS

1 Pour the water and oil into the bread pan. Reverse the order in which you add the liquid and dry ingredients, if necessary. Add the flour, making sure it covers the water.

2 Add the salt and sugar in separate corners of the pan. Make a shallow indent in the centre of the flour and add the yeast. Set the bread machine to the dough setting; use basic or pizza dough setting (if available). Press Start.

*These well-known flatbreads are easy to make and extremely versatile.
Serve them warm with dips or soups, or split them in half and stuff the
pockets with your favourite vegetable, meat or cheese filling.*

3 When the dough cycle has finished, remove the dough from the machine. Place it on a lightly floured surface and knock back (punch down) gently.

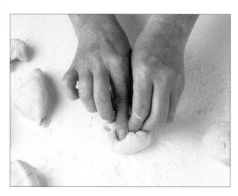

4 Divide the dough into six or ten equal-size pieces, depending on whether you want large or small pitta breads. Shape each piece into a ball.

5 Cover the balls of dough with oiled clear film (plastic wrap) and leave to rest for about 10 minutes. Preheat the oven to 230°C/450°F/Gas 8. Then place three baking sheets in the oven to heat.

6 Flatten each piece of dough slightly, and then roll out into an oval or round, about 5mm/¼in thick.

7 Lightly sprinkle each pitta with extra flour. Cover with oiled clear film and leave to rest for 10 minutes.

8 Place the pittas on the baking sheets and bake for 5–6 minutes, or until they are puffed up and lightly browned. Transfer the pitta breads on to wire racks to cool.

200ml/7fl oz/⅞ cup water
250g/9oz/2¼ cups unbleached strong white (bread) flour
75g/3oz/¾ cup semolina
5ml/1 tsp aniseed (anise seed)
7.5ml/1½ tsp salt
2.5ml/½ tsp granulated sugar
5ml/1 tsp easy-blend (rapid-rise) dried yeast
olive oil, for brushing
sesame seeds, for sprinkling

MAKES 2 FLATBREADS

1 Pour the water into the machine pan. Reverse the order in which you add the wet and dry ingredients if necessary.

2 Add the flour, semolina and aniseed, covering the water. Place the salt and sugar in separate corners. Make an indent in the flour and add the yeast. Set the machine to the dough setting; use the basic dough setting if available.

MOROCCAN KSRA

This leavened flatbread is made with semolina and spiced with aniseed. It is the traditional accompaniment to tagine, a spicy Moroccan stew, but is equally good with salad, cheeses or dips. It can be served warm or cold.

3 Press Start on your bread machine, then lightly flour two baking sheets. When the cycle has finished, place the dough on a lightly floured surface.

4 Knock back (punch down) gently, shape into two balls, then flatten into 2cm/¾in thick discs. Place each dough disc on a baking sheet.

5 Cover the dough discs with oiled clear film (plastic wrap) and leave to rise for 30 minutes, or until doubled in bulk.

6 Preheat the oven to 200°C/400°F/Gas 6. Brush the top of each piece of dough with olive oil and sprinkle with sesame seeds. Prick the surface with a skewer.

7 Bake for about 20–25 minutes, or until the ksra are golden and sound hollow when tapped underneath. Turn out on to a wire rack to cool.

VARIATION
Replace up to half the strong white flour with strong wholemeal (whole-wheat) flour for a nuttier flavour.

240ml/8½fl oz/generous 1 cup water
30ml/2 tbsp olive oil
450g/1lb/4 cups unbleached strong white (bread) flour
5ml/1 tsp salt
5ml/1 tsp sugar
5ml/1 tsp easy-blend (rapid-rise) dried yeast
1 egg yolk mixed with 10ml/2 tsp water, for glazing
nigella or poppy seeds, for sprinkling

MAKES 3 FLATBREADS

1 Pour the water and olive oil into the bread machine pan. If the instructions for your machine specify that the yeast is to be placed in the pan first, reverse the order in which you add the liquid and dry ingredients.

2 Sprinkle in the flour, making sure that it covers the liquid. Add the salt in one corner of the bread pan and the sugar in another corner. Make a small indent in the centre of the flour; add the yeast.

PIDE

A traditional Turkish ridged flatbread, this is often baked plain, but can also be sprinkled with aromatic black nigella seeds, which taste rather like oregano. If you can't find nigella seeds, use poppy seeds.

3 Set the bread machine to the dough setting; use basic dough setting (if available). Press Start.

4 When the dough cycle has finished, remove the pide dough from the bread machine and place it on a surface lightly dusted with flour. Knock back (punch down) gently and divide it into three equal-size pieces. Shape each piece of dough into a ball.

5 Roll each ball of dough into a round, about 15cm/6in in diameter. Cover with oiled clear film (plastic wrap) and leave to rise for 20 minutes. Meanwhile, preheat the oven to 230°C/450°F/Gas 8.

6 Using your fingers, ridge the bread, while enlarging it until it is 5mm/¼in thick. Start from the top of the round, pressing your fingers down and away from you, into the bread. Repeat a second row beneath the first row, and continue down the bread.

7 Turn the bread by 90 degrees and repeat the pressing to give a criss-cross ridged effect. Place the pide on floured baking sheets, brush with egg glaze and sprinkle with nigella or poppy seeds. Bake for 9–10 minutes, or until puffy and golden. Serve immediately.

OLIVE FOUGASSE

A French hearth bread, fougasse is traditionally baked on the floor of the hot bread oven, just after the fire has been raked out. It can be left plain or flavoured with olives, herbs, nuts or cheese.

210ml/7½fl oz/scant 1 cup water
15ml/1 tbsp olive oil, plus extra
for brushing
350g/12oz/3 cups unbleached strong
white (bread) flour
5ml/1 tsp salt
5ml/1 tsp granulated sugar
5ml/1 tsp easy-blend (rapid-rise)
dried yeast
50g/2oz/½ cup pitted black
olives, chopped

MAKES 1 FLATBREAD

1 Pour the water and the olive oil into the bread machine pan. Reverse the order in which you add the wet and dry ingredients if necessary.

2 Sprinkle in the flour, making sure that it covers the liquid. Add the salt in one corner of the bread pan and the sugar in another corner. Make a small indent in the centre of the flour, but not down as far as the liquid, and add the yeast.

3 Set the bread machine to the dough setting; use basic or pizza dough setting (if available). Press Start. When the cycle has finished, remove the dough from the machine and place it on a lightly floured surface.

4 Knock back (punch down) the dough gently and flatten it slightly. Sprinkle over the olives and fold over the dough two or three times to incorporate them.

5 Flatten the dough and roll it into an oblong, about 30cm/12in long. With a sharp knife make four or five parallel cuts diagonally through the body of the dough, but leaving the edges intact. Gently stretch the fougasse dough so that it resembles a ladder.

6 Lightly oil a baking sheet, then place the shaped dough on it. Cover with oiled clear film (plastic wrap) and leave in a warm place for 30 minutes, or until the dough has nearly doubled in bulk.

7 Preheat the oven to 220°C/425°F/ Gas 7. Brush the top of the fougasse with olive oil, place in the oven and bake about for 20–25 minutes, or until the bread is golden. Turn out on to a wire rack to cool.

ONION FOCACCIA

Focaccia, with its characteristic texture and dimpled surface, has become hugely popular in recent years. This version has a delectable red onion and fresh sage topping.

210ml/7½fl oz/scant 1 cup water
15ml/1 tbsp olive oil
350g/12oz/3 cups unbleached strong white (bread) flour
2.5ml/½ tsp salt
5ml/1 tsp granulated sugar
5ml/1 tsp easy-blend (rapid-rise) dried yeast
15ml/1 tbsp chopped fresh sage
15ml/1 tbsp chopped red onion

FOR THE TOPPING
30ml/2 tbsp olive oil
½ red onion, thinly sliced
5 fresh sage leaves
10ml/2 tsp coarse sea salt
coarsely ground black pepper

MAKES 1 FLATBREAD

7 Meanwhile, preheat the oven to 200°C/400°F/Gas 6. Uncover the risen focaccia and, using your fingertips, poke the dough to make deep dimples over the surface. Cover and leave to rise for 10–15 minutes, or until the dough has doubled in bulk.

8 Drizzle over the olive oil and sprinkle with the onion, sage leaves, sea salt and black pepper. Bake for 20–25 minutes, or until golden. Turn out on to a wire rack to cool slightly. Serve warm.

1 Pour the water and oil into the bread pan. Reverse the order in which you add the wet and dry ingredients if necessary.

2 Sprinkle in the flour, making sure that it covers the liquid. Add the salt and sugar in separate corners. Make a small indent in the flour and add the yeast.

3 Set the bread machine to the dough setting. If your machine has a choice of settings use the basic or pizza dough setting. Press Start.

4 Lightly oil a 25–28cm/10–11in shallow round cake tin (pan) or pizza pan. When the cycle has finished, remove the dough from the pan and place it on a surface lightly dusted with flour.

5 Knock back (punch down) and flatten it slightly. Sprinkle on the sage and red onion and knead gently to incorporate.

6 Shape the dough into a ball, flatten it, then roll it into a 25–28cm/10–11in round. Place in the prepared tin. Cover with oiled clear film (plastic wrap) and leave in a warm place for 20 minutes.

TOMATO AND PROSCIUTTO PIZZA

This combination of fresh plum tomatoes, sun-dried tomatoes, garlic and prosciutto with three cheeses is truly mouthwatering. Pizzas provide the perfect opportunity for exercising your individuality, so experiment with different topping ingredients if you like.

SMALL AND MEDIUM
MAKES ONE 30CM/12IN PIZZA
140ml/5fl oz/⅝ cup water
15ml/1 tbsp extra virgin olive oil
225g/8oz/2 cups unbleached strong white (bread) flour
5ml/1 tsp salt
2.5ml/½ tsp granulated sugar
2.5ml/½ tsp easy-blend (rapid-rise) dried yeast

FOR THE FILLING
45ml/3 tbsp sun-dried tomato paste
150g/5½oz mozzarella cheese, sliced
4 fresh plum tomatoes, about 400g/14oz, coarsely chopped
1 small yellow (bell) pepper, halved, seeded and cut into thin strips
50g/2oz prosciutto, torn into pieces
8 fresh basil leaves
4 large garlic cloves, halved
50g/2oz feta cheese, crumbled
30ml/2 tbsp extra virgin olive oil
30ml/2 tbsp freshly grated Parmesan cheese
salt and freshly ground black pepper

LARGE
MAKES TWO 30CM/12IN PIZZAS
280ml/10fl oz/1¼ cups water
30ml/2 tbsp extra virgin olive oil
450g/1lb/4 cups unbleached strong white flour
7.5ml/1½ tsp salt
2.5ml/½tsp granulated sugar
5ml/1 tsp easy-blend dried yeast

FOR THE FILLING
90ml/6 tbsp sun-dried tomato paste
300g/11oz mozzarella cheese, sliced
8 fresh plum tomatoes, about 800g/1¾lb, coarsely chopped
1 large yellow pepper, halved, seeded and cut into thin strips
115g/4oz prosciutto, torn into pieces
16 fresh basil leaves
8 large garlic cloves, halved
115g/4oz feta cheese, crumbled
45ml/3 tbsp extra virgin olive oil
60ml/4 tbsp freshly grated Parmesan cheese
salt and freshly ground black pepper

1 Pour the water and olive oil into the bread machine pan. If the instructions for your machine specify that the yeast is to be placed in the pan first, reverse the order in which you add the liquid and dry ingredients.

2 Sprinkle in the flour, making sure that it covers the liquid. Add the salt in one corner of the bread pan and the sugar in another corner. Make a small indent in the centre of the flour, then add the yeast.

3 Set the bread machine to the dough setting; use basic or pizza dough setting (if available). Press Start. Lightly oil one or two pizza pans or baking sheets.

4 When the dough cycle has finished, remove the dough from the machine and place it on a lightly floured surface. Knock back (punch down) gently. If making the larger quantity divide the dough into two equal pieces. Preheat the oven to 220°C/425°F/Gas 7.

5 Roll out the pizza dough into one or two 30cm/12in rounds. Place in the prepared pan(s) or on the baking sheet(s). Spread the sun-dried tomato paste over the pizza base(s) and arrange two-thirds of the mozzarella slices on top.

6 Sprinkle with the chopped tomatoes, pepper strips, prosciutto, whole basil leaves, garlic, remaining mozzarella and feta. Drizzle over the olive oil and sprinkle with the Parmesan. Season with salt and pepper. Bake the pizza for 15–20 minutes, or until golden and sizzling. Serve immediately.

VARIATION
This topping lends itself particularly well to the nutty flavour of a wholemeal (whole-wheat) pizza base. Replace half the strong white flour with strong wholemeal flour. You may need to add a little more water as wholemeal flour absorbs more liquid.

100ml/3½fl oz/7 tbsp water
1 egg
225g/8oz/2 cups unbleached strong
white (bread) flour
5ml/1 tsp salt
25g/1oz/2 tbsp butter
5ml/1 tsp easy-blend (rapid-rise)
dried yeast

For the Filling
60ml/4 tbsp olive oil
575g/1¼lb onions, thinly sliced
15ml/1 tbsp Dijon mustard
3–4 tomatoes, about 280g/10oz, peeled
and sliced
10ml/2 tsp chopped fresh basil
12 drained canned anchovies
12 black olives
salt and freshly ground black pepper

SERVES 6

1 Pour the water and egg into the bread machine pan. If the instructions for your machine specify that the yeast is to be placed in the pan first, then reverse the order in which you add the liquid and the dry ingredients.

2 Sprinkle in the strong white flour, making sure that it completely covers the water and the egg. Add the salt in one corner of the pan and the butter in another corner. Make a small indent in the centre of the flour, but not down as far as the liquid, and add the easy-blend dried yeast.

3 Set the bread machine to the dough setting; use basic or pizza dough setting (if available). Press Start. Lightly oil a 27 x 20cm/11 x 8in Swiss (jelly) roll tin (pan) that is about 1cm/½in deep.

PISSALADIÈRE

This French version of an Italian pizza is typical of Niçoise dishes, with anchovies and olives providing the distinctive flavour typical of the region.

4 Make the filling. Heat the olive oil in a large frying pan and cook the onions over a low heat for about 20 minutes, until very soft. Set aside to cool.

5 When the dough cycle has finished, remove the dough from the machine and place it on a lightly floured surface. Knock back (punch down) gently, then roll it out to a 30 x 23cm/12 x 9in rectangle. Place in the prepared tin, and press outwards and upwards, so that the dough covers the base and sides.

6 Spread the mustard over the dough. Arrange the tomato slices on top. Season the onions with salt, pepper and basil and spread the mixture over the tomatoes.

7 Arrange the anchovies in a lattice and dot with the black olives. Cover with oiled clear film (plastic wrap) and leave to rise for 10–15 minutes. Meanwhile preheat the oven to 200°C/400°F/Gas 6. Bake the pissaladière for 25–30 minutes, or until the base is cooked and golden around the edges. Serve hot or warm.

SICILIAN SFINCIONE

Sfincione is the Sicilian equivalent of pizza. The Sicilians insist they were making these tasty snacks long before pizzas were made in mainland Italy.

1 Pour the water and oil into the bread pan. If your instructions specify that the yeast is to be placed in the bread pan first, reverse the order in which you add the liquid and the dry ingredients.

2 Sprinkle in the flour, making sure that it covers the liquid. Add the salt in one corner of the bread pan and the sugar in another corner. Make a small indent in the centre of the flour; add the yeast.

3 Set the bread machine to the dough setting; use basic or pizza dough setting (if available). Press Start. Then lightly oil two baking sheets.

4 Make the topping. Peel and chop the tomatoes. Put in a bowl, add the garlic and 15ml/1 tbsp of the olive oil and toss together. Heat the sunflower oil in a small pan and sauté the onions until softened. Set aside to cool.

5 When the dough cycle has finished, remove the dough from the machine and place it on a lightly floured surface. Knock back (punch down) gently and divide it into four equal pieces.

6 Roll each piece of dough out to a round, each about 15–18cm/6–7in in diameter. Space the rounds well apart on the prepared baking sheets, then push up the dough edges on each to make a thin rim. Cover the sfincione with oiled clear film (plastic wrap) and leave to rise for 10 minutes. Meanwhile, preheat the oven to 220°C/425°F/Gas 7.

7 Sprinkle the topping over the bases, ending with the Pecorino. Season, then drizzle with the remaining olive oil.

8 Bake near the top of the oven for 15–20 minutes or until the base of each sfincione is cooked. Serve immediately.

200ml/7fl oz/⅞ cup water
30ml/2 tbsp extra virgin olive oil
350g/12oz/3 cups unbleached strong white (bread) flour
7.5ml/1½ tsp salt
2.5ml/½ tsp granulated sugar
5ml/1 tsp easy-blend (rapid-rise) dried yeast

FOR THE TOPPING
6 tomatoes
2 garlic cloves, chopped
45ml/3 tbsp olive oil
15ml/1 tbsp sunflower oil
2 onions, chopped
8 pitted black olives, chopped
10ml/2 tsp dried oregano
90ml/6 tbsp freshly grated Pecorino cheese
salt and freshly ground black pepper

MAKES 4 SFINCIONE

130ml/4½fl oz/generous ½ cup water
30ml/2 tbsp extra virgin olive oil,
plus extra for brushing
225g/8oz/2 cups unbleached strong
white (bread) flour
5ml/1 tsp salt
2.5ml/½ tsp granulated sugar
5ml/1 tsp easy-blend (rapid-rise)
dried yeast

FOR THE FILLING
75g/3oz salami, in one piece
50g/2oz/½ cup drained sun-dried
tomatoes in olive oil, chopped
100g/4oz/⅔ cup mozzarella
cheese, cubed
50g/2oz/⅔ cup freshly grated
Parmesan cheese
50g/2oz Gorgonzola cheese, cubed
75g/3oz/scant ½ cup ricotta cheese
30ml/3 tbsp chopped fresh basil
2 egg yolks
salt and freshly ground black pepper

MAKES 2 CALZONE

1 Pour the water and olive oil into the bread pan. Reverse the order in which you add the liquid and dry ingredients if this is necessary for your machine. Sprinkle in the white bread flour, making sure that it covers the liquid.

VARIATIONS
The ingredients for the filling can be varied, depending on what you have in the refrigerator, and to suit personal tastes. Replace the salami with ham or sautéed mushrooms. Add a chopped fresh chilli for a more piquant version. Make four individual calzones instead of two large ones.

CALZONE

Calzone is an enclosed pizza, with the filling inside. It originates from Naples and was originally made from a rectangular piece of pizza dough, unlike the modern version, which looks like a large Cornish pasty.

2 Add the salt and sugar in separate corners of the bread pan. Make a small indent in the centre of the flour, but not down as far as the liquid, and add the easy-blend dried yeast.

3 Set the bread machine to the dough setting; use basic or pizza dough setting (if available). Press Start.

4 To make the topping, cut the salami into 5mm/¼in dice. Put the dice in a bowl and add the sun-dried tomatoes, mozzarella, Parmesan, Gorgonzola and ricotta cheeses, basil and egg yolks. Mix well and season to taste with salt and plenty of ground black pepper. Lightly oil a large baking sheet.

5 When the cycle has finished, remove the calzone dough from the bread pan and place it on a lightly floured surface. Knock back (punch down) gently, then divide the dough into two equal pieces. Roll out each piece of dough into a flat round, about 5mm/¼in thick. Preheat the oven to 220°C/425°F/Gas 7.

COOK'S TIP
Calzone can be made in advance. Make the dough, transfer to a bowl, cover with oiled clear film (plastic wrap) and store in the refrigerator for up to 4 hours. Knock back (punch down) if it starts to rise to the top of the bowl. Bring back to room temperature, then continue with shaping and filling. If you like, shape and fill up to 2 hours before baking. Place the calzone in the refrigerator until you are ready to bake them.

6 Divide the filling between the two pieces of dough, placing it on one half only, in each case. Leave a 1.5cm/½in border of the dough all round.

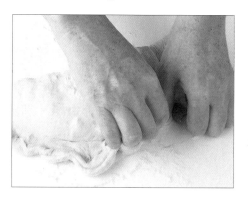

7 Dampen the edges of each dough round with water, fold the remaining dough over the filling and then crimp the edges of each calzone with your fingers to seal securely.

8 Place the calzone on the baking sheet, brush with olive oil and bake for 20 minutes, or until golden.

SOURDOUGHS AND STARTER DOUGH BREADS

Breads made with starters acquire their wonderful textures and flavours from the multiple ferments and starter doughs. The bread machine provides the perfect environment to nurture these doughs. This section also includes a recipe for bread made with fresh yeast.

15g/½oz fresh yeast
5ml/1 tsp granulated sugar
260ml/9fl oz/1⅛ cups water
30ml/2 tbsp sunflower oil
450g/1lb/4 cups unbleached strong
white (bread) flour
30ml/2 tbsp skimmed milk powder
(non fat dry milk)
10ml/2 tsp salt
75ml/5 tbsp sunflower seeds,
for coating

MAKES 1 LOAF

1 In a small bowl, cream the fresh yeast with the sugar and 30ml/2 tbsp of the water. Leave to stand for 5 minutes, then scrape the mixture into the bread machine pan. Add the remaining water and the sunflower oil. However, if the instructions for your bread machine specify that the yeast is to be placed in the pan first, simply reverse the order in which you add the liquid and dry ingredients to the pan.

2 Sprinkle in the flour, making sure that it covers the water completely. Add the skimmed milk powder and salt to the bread pan.

3 Set the bread machine to the dough setting; use basic dough setting (if available). Press Start, then lightly oil a baking sheet.

4 When the dough cycle has finished, remove the dough from the machine and place it on a lightly floured surface. Knock back (punch down) gently, and then knead for 2–3 minutes. Roll the dough into a ball and pat it into a plump round cushion shape.

FRESH YEAST BREAD

If you particularly like the flavour of fresh yeast, try this recipe. Bread machine manufacturers do not recommend using fresh yeast for bread baked in their appliances, but if the bread is to be baked in the oven, the machine can be used to prepare the dough.

5 Sprinkle the sunflower seeds on a clean area of work surface and roll the loaf in them until evenly coated. Place on the prepared baking sheet. Cover with lightly oiled clear film (plastic wrap) and leave to rise in a warm place for 30–45 minutes, or until the loaf has doubled in size.

6 Meanwhile, preheat the oven to 230°C/450°F/Gas 8. Cut two slashes, one on each side of the loaf, then cut two slashes at right angles to the first to make a grid pattern.

7 Bake the loaf for 15 minutes, then reduce the oven temperature to 200°C/400°F/Gas 6. Bake for 20 minutes more, or until the bread sounds hollow when tapped on the base. Turn out on to a wire rack to cool.

COOK'S TIP
This makes a basic fresh yeast bread which you can shape or flavour to suit yourself. Leave out the sunflower seeds, if you like.

SCHIACCIATA CON UVA

A Tuscan bread baked to celebrate the grape harvest. The fresh grapes on top are the new crop, while the raisins inside symbolize last year's gathering-in.

FOR THE STARTER
200ml/7fl oz/⅞ cup water
175g/6oz/1½ cups organic strong
white (bread) flour
1.5ml/¼ tsp easy-blend (rapid-rise)
dried yeast

FOR THE SCHIACCIATA DOUGH
200g/7oz/generous 1 cup raisins
150ml/5fl oz/⅔ cup Italian red wine,
such as Chianti
45ml/3 tbsp extra virgin olive oil
45ml/3 tbsp water
280g/10oz/2½ cups unbleached strong
white flour
50g/2oz/¼ cup granulated sugar
7.5ml/1½ tsp salt
5ml/1 tsp easy-blend dried yeast

FOR THE TOPPING
280g/10oz small black
seedless grapes
30ml/2 tbsp demerara (raw) sugar

MAKES 1 LOAF

1 Pour the water for the starter into the bread machine pan. If the instructions for your machine specify that the yeast is to be placed in the pan first, reverse the order in which you add the liquid and dry ingredients.

2 Sprinkle in the organic flour, making sure that it completely covers the water. Make a small indent in the centre of the flour, but not down as far as the liquid, and add the easy-blend dried yeast. Set the bread machine to the dough setting; use basic dough setting (if available). Press Start. Mix the starter for 5 minutes, then switch off the machine and set aside.

3 Leave the starter to ferment inside the machine for 24 hours. Do not lift the lid. If you need the machine, transfer the starter to a bowl, cover it with a damp dishtowel and leave it to stand at room temperature.

4 Place the raisins for the dough in a small pan. Add the wine and heat gently until warm. Cover and set aside.

5 Remove the bread pan from the machine. Return the starter to the pan, if necessary, and pour in the oil and water. Sprinkle in the flour. Add the sugar and salt in separate corners. Make a shallow indent in the centre of the flour and add the yeast.

6 Set the bread machine to the dough setting. If your machine has a choice of settings, use the basic dough setting. Press Start. Lightly oil a baking sheet.

7 When the dough cycle has finished, remove the dough from the machine and place it on a lightly floured surface. Knock back (punch down) gently, then divide it in half. Roll each piece out into a round, about 1cm/½in thick. Place one round on the prepared baking sheet.

8 Spread the raisins over the dough. Place the remaining piece of dough on top and pinch the edges together to seal. Cover with lightly oiled clear film (plastic wrap) and leave to rise in a warm place for 30–45 minutes, or until it is almost doubled in size.

9 Meanwhile, preheat the oven to 190°C/ 375°F/Gas 5. Cover the schiacciata with the fresh black grapes, pressing them lightly into the dough. Sprinkle with the sugar. Bake for 40 minutes, or until the bread is golden and sounds hollow when tapped on the base. Turn out on to a wire rack to cool slightly before serving.

FRENCH COURONNE

This crown-shaped loaf is made with a chef starter, which is fermented for at least 2 days and up to a week; the longer it is left the more it will develop the characteristic sourdough flavour.

FOR THE CHEF
0.6ml/⅛ tsp easy-blend (rapid-rise) dried yeast
50g/2oz/½ cup organic strong white (bread) flour
45ml/3 tbsp water

FOR THE FIRST REFRESHMENT
65ml/4½ tbsp water
115g/4oz/1 cup organic strong white flour

FOR THE LEVAIN
115ml/4fl oz/½ cup water
115g/4oz/1 cup organic strong white flour

FOR THE COURONNE DOUGH
240ml/8½fl oz/generous 1 cup cold water
325g/11½oz/scant 3 cups unbleached strong white flour
7.5ml/1½ tsp salt
5ml/1 tsp granulated sugar
2.5ml/½ tsp easy-blend dried yeast

MAKES 1 LOAF

1 Mix the yeast and organic strong white flour for the chef in a small bowl. Add the water and gradually mix to a stiff dough with a metal spoon. Cover with oiled clear film (plastic wrap) and set aside in a warm place for 2–3 days.

2 Break open the crust on the chef – the middle should be aerated and sweet smelling. Mix in the water and flour for the first refreshment, stirring to form a fairly stiff dough. Replace the clear film cover and set aside for a further 2 days in a warm place.

3 Transfer the chef to the machine pan. If the instructions for your machine specify that the yeast is to be placed in the pan first, reverse the order in which you add the liquid and dry ingredients.

4 Add the water for the levain. Sprinkle in the flour, making sure that it covers the water. Set the bread machine to the dough setting; use basic dough setting (if available). Press Start.

5 When the dough cycle has finished, switch the machine off, leaving the levain inside. Do not lift the lid. Leave the levain for 8 hours. If you need the machine, transfer the levain to a bowl, cover it with a damp dishtowel and leave it at room temperature.

6 Take the bread pan out of the machine. Remove about half of the levain from the pan. If the levain is in a bowl, put 200g/7oz/scant 1 cup of it back in the pan. Reserve the spare levain to replenish and use for your next loaf of bread. Meanwhile pour the water for the dough into the bread pan. Sprinkle in the flour. Add the salt and sugar, placing them in separate corners of the bread pan. Make a small indent in the centre of the flour and add the yeast.

7 Set the bread machine to the dough setting; use basic dough setting (if available). Press Start. Lightly oil a baking sheet.

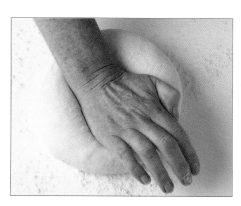

8 When the dough cycle has finished, remove the dough from the machine and place it on a lightly floured surface. Knock back (punch down) gently, then shape it into a ball and make a hole in the centre with the heel of your hand. Gradually enlarge this cavity, using your fingertips and turning the dough, then use both hands to stretch the dough gently into a large doughnut shape. The cavity should measure 13–15cm/5–6in.

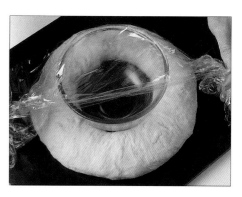

9 Place the shaped dough on the prepared baking sheet. Fit a small bowl into the centre to prevent the dough from filling in the hole when it rises. Cover it with lightly oiled clear film and leave it in a warm place for an hour, or until almost doubled in size.

10 Preheat the oven to 230°C/450°F/ Gas 8. Dust the loaf with extra flour and make four slashes at equal intervals around the couronne. Bake for 35–40 minutes, or until the bread is golden and sounds hollow when tapped on its base. Turn out on to a wire rack to cool.

FOR THE STARTER
175ml/6fl oz/¾ cup milk
115g/4oz/1 cup rye flour
4ml/¾ tsp easy-blend (rapid-rise)
dried yeast

FOR THE DOUGH
170ml/6fl oz/scant ¾ cup flat beer
300g/10½oz/2¾ cups unbleached
strong white (bread) flour
85g/3oz/¾ cup rye flour
15ml/1 tbsp clear honey
7.5ml/1½ tsp salt
2.5ml/½ tsp easy-blend dried yeast
flour for dusting

MAKES 1 LOAF

1 Mix the milk, flour and yeast for the starter in a bowl. Stir, then cover with a damp dishtowel. Rest in a warm place for 3 days; stir once a day.

2 Make the dough. Tip the starter into the bread machine pan and add the beer. If the instructions for your machine specify that the yeast is to be placed in the pan first, simply reverse the order in which you add the liquid and dry ingredients.

3 Sprinkle in the white and rye flours, making sure that the beer is completely covered. Add the honey and salt, placing them in separate corners of the bread pan. Make a small indent in the centre of the flour, but not down as far as the liquid, and add the yeast.

4 Set the bread machine to the dough setting; use basic dough setting (if available). Press Start. Lightly oil a fairly deep 17cm/6½in square tin (pan).

HONEY AND BEER RYE BREAD

The flavour of this rye bread is enhanced by leaving the sourdough starter to develop over 3 days as a prelude to making the dough.

5 When the dough cycle has finished, remove the dough from the machine and place it on a lightly floured surface. Knock back (punch down) gently.

6 Roll the dough into a rectangle about 2cm/¾in thick. It needs to be the same width as the tin and three times as long. Fold the bottom third of the dough up and the top third down, then seal the edges with the rolling pin.

7 Place the folded dough in the prepared tin, cover it with lightly oiled clear film (plastic wrap) and leave in a warm place for 45–60 minutes, or until the dough has risen almost to the top of the tin.

8 Meanwhile, preheat the oven to 220°C/425°F/Gas 7. Dust the top of the loaf with a little flour to give a rustic-looking appearance.

9 Using a sharp knife slash the loaf with four long cuts. Repeat with five cuts in the opposite direction to give a cross-hatched effect.

10 Bake the bread for 30–35 minutes, or until it sounds hollow when tapped on the base. Turn out on to a wire rack to cool slightly before serving.

PANE ALL'OLIO

Italians love to use olive oil in cooking, as this bread amply proves. The combined flavours of the olive oil and the biga starter give a rich, earthy and yeasty flavour to the bread.

FOR THE BIGA
105ml/7 tbsp water
175g/6oz/1½ cups strong white (bread) flour
5ml/1 tsp easy-blend (rapid-rise) dried yeast

FOR THE DOUGH
90ml/6 tbsp water
60ml/4 tbsp extra virgin olive oil
225g/8oz/2 cups unbleached strong white (bread) flour
10ml/2 tsp salt
5ml/1 tsp granulated sugar

MAKES 1 LOAF

COOK'S TIP
If you haven't got a baking stone, you can use unglazed terracotta tiles placed edge to edge. Make sure that the air can flow around the edges.

1 Pour the water for the biga into the bread machine pan. If the instructions for your machine specify that the yeast is to be placed in the pan first, reverse the order in which you add the liquid and dry ingredients.

2 Sprinkle in the flour, covering the water. Make a shallow indent in the centre of the flour and add the yeast.

3 Set the machine to the dough setting; use basic dough setting (if available). Press Start. When the dough cycle has finished, switch the machine off, but leave the biga inside, with the lid closed, for 8 hours. If you need the machine during this time, transfer the biga to a bowl, cover it with a damp dishtowel and leave it at room temperature.

4 Remove the bread pan from the machine. Break the biga into three or four pieces. If you took it out of the bread pan, put it back.

5 Pour in the water and olive oil for the dough. Sprinkle in the flour, covering the liquid. Add the salt and sugar in separate corners of the bread pan.

6 Set the bread machine to the dough setting; use basic dough setting (if available). Press Start. Lightly flour a peel (baker's shovel) or baking sheet.

7 When the dough cycle has finished, place the dough on a lightly floured surface. Knock back (punch down) gently, then shape it into a plump round.

8 Using the palms of your hands, gently roll the dough backwards and forwards, concentrating on the ends, until it forms a tapered, torpedo-shaped loaf about 30cm/12in long. Place the loaf on the prepared peel or baking sheet and cover it with lightly oiled clear film (plastic wrap). Leave it to rise in a warm place for 45–60 minutes, or until the dough has almost doubled in size.

9 Meanwhile, place a baking stone on a shelf about a third of the way up from the bottom of the oven. Preheat the oven to 230°C/450°F/Gas 8. Dust the top of the bread lightly with flour and slash it along its length. Transfer the bread to the hot baking stone.

10 Mist the inside of the oven with water. Bake the loaf for 15 minutes, misting the oven again after 2 minutes and then after 4 minutes. Reduce the oven temperature to 190°C/375°F/Gas 5 and bake the loaf for 20–25 minutes more, or until it is golden all over and the bread sounds hollow when tapped on the base. Turn out on to a wire rack before serving warm or cooled.

FOR THE POOLISH
200ml/7fl oz/⅞ cup water
175g/6oz/1½ cups unbleached strong
white (bread) flour
50g/2oz/½ cup strong wholemeal
(whole-wheat) flour
1.5ml/¼ tsp easy-blend (rapid-rise)
dried yeast

FOR THE DOUGH
120ml/4fl oz/½ cup water
225g/8oz/2 cups unbleached strong
white flour
50g/2oz/½ cup strong wholemeal flour
25g/1oz/¼ cup rye flour
7.5ml/1½ tsp salt
2.5ml/½ tsp granulated sugar
2.5ml/½ tsp easy-blend dried yeast

MAKES 1 LOAF

PAIN DE CAMPAGNE

——

This rustic-style French bread is made using a poolish or sponge. The fermentation period is fairly short, which makes for a loaf which is not as sour as some breads of this type. It is also lighter and slightly less chewy.

1 Pour the water for the poolish into the bread machine pan. If the instructions for your machine specify that the yeast is to be placed in the pan first, reverse the order in which you add the liquid and dry ingredients.

2 Sprinkle in both types of flour, making sure that the water is completely covered. Make a small indent in the centre of the flour; add the yeast. Set the bread machine to the dough setting; use basic dough setting (if available). Press Start.

3 When the dough cycle has finished, switch the machine off, but leave the poolish inside, with the lid closed, for 2–8 hours, depending on how sour you like your bread to taste.

4 Remove the bread pan from the machine. Pour in the water for the dough. Sprinkle in each type of flour, then add the salt and sugar in separate corners. Make a small indent in the centre of the flour; add the yeast. Set the bread machine to the dough setting. If your machine has a choice of settings, use the basic dough setting. Press Start.

5 When the dough cycle has finished, place the dough on a lightly floured surface. Knock back (punch down) gently, then shape it into a plump ball. Place on a lightly oiled baking sheet.

6 Cover with lightly oiled clear film (plastic wrap) and leave to rise in a warm place for 30–45 minutes, or until the dough has almost doubled in bulk. Preheat the oven to 220°C/425°F/Gas 7.

7 Dust the top of the loaf with flour. Cut three parallel slashes across the loaf, then cut three more slashes at right angles to the first set.

8 Transfer the baking sheet to a rack near the bottom of the oven and bake the bread for 40 minutes, or until it is golden and sounds hollow when tapped on the base. Turn out on to a wire rack.

CIABATTA

This popular flat loaf is irregularly shaped and typically has large air holes in the crumb. The dough for this bread is extremely wet. Do not be tempted to add more flour – it's meant to be that way.

FOR THE BIGA
200ml/7fl oz/⅞ cup water
175g/6oz/1½ cups unbleached strong white (bread) flour
2.5ml/½ tsp easy-blend (rapid-rise) dried yeast

FOR THE CIABATTA DOUGH
200ml/7fl oz/⅞ cup water
30ml/2 tbsp milk
30ml/2 tbsp extra virgin olive oil
325g/11½oz/scant 3 cups unbleached strong white flour,
plus extra for dusting
7.5ml/1½ tsp salt
2.5ml/½ tsp granulated sugar
1.5ml/¼ tsp easy-blend dried yeast

MAKES 2 LOAVES

1 Pour the water for the biga into the bread pan. If necessary, reverse the order in which you add the liquid and dry ingredients. Sprinkle in the flour, covering the water. Make an indent in the centre of the flour; add the yeast.

2 Set the bread machine to the dough setting; use basic dough setting (if available). Press Start. Mix for 5 minutes, then switch off the machine.

3 Leave the biga in the bread machine, or place in a large bowl covered with lightly oiled clear film (plastic wrap), for at least 12 hours, until the dough has risen and is starting to collapse.

4 Return the biga to the pan, if necessary. Add the water, milk and oil for the ciabatta dough. Sprinkle in the flour. Add the salt and sugar in separate corners. Make a small indent in the centre of the flour and add the yeast.

5 Set the bread machine to the dough setting; use the basic dough setting (if available). Press Start.

6 When the cycle has finished, transfer the dough to a bowl and cover with oiled clear film. Leave to rise for about 1 hour, until the dough has trebled in size. Sprinkle two baking sheets with flour.

7 Using a spoon or a dough scraper, divide the dough into two portions. Carefully tip one portion of the dough on to one of the prepared baking sheets, trying to avoid knocking the air out of the dough. Using well-floured hands shape the dough into a rectangular loaf about 2.5cm/1in thick, pulling and stretching as necessary. Repeat with the remaining piece of dough.

8 Sprinkle both loaves with flour. Leave them, uncovered, in a warm place for about 20–30 minutes. The dough will spread and rise. Meanwhile, preheat the oven to 220°C/425°F/Gas 7.

9 Bake the ciabatta for 25–30 minutes, or until both loaves have risen, are light golden in colour and sound hollow when tapped on the base. Transfer them to a wire rack to cool before serving with butter, or olive oil for dipping.

For the Chef
200ml/7fl oz/⅞ cup water
175g/6oz/1½ cups rye flour
1.5ml/¼ tsp easy-blend (rapid-rise)
dried yeast

For the First Refreshment
70ml/2½fl oz/¼ cup + 1 tbsp water
50g/2oz/½ cup plain (all-purpose) flour

For the Second Refreshment
15ml/1 tbsp water
50g/2oz/½ cup plain flour

For the Bread Dough
15ml/1 tbsp water
225g/8oz/2 cups unbleached strong
white (bread) flour
10ml/2 tsp salt
5ml/1 tsp clear honey
2.5ml/½ tsp easy-blend dried yeast
unbleached strong white flour,
for dusting

Makes 1 Loaf

1 Pour the water for the chef into the bread machine pan. If the instructions for your machine specify that the yeast is to be placed in the pan first, reverse the order in which you add the liquid and dry ingredients.

2 Sprinkle in the rye flour, making sure that it covers the water completely. Make a small indent in the centre of the flour, but not down as far as the liquid, and add the easy-blend dried yeast. Set the bread machine to the dough setting; use basic dough setting (if available). Press Start. Mix the dough for about 10 minutes, and then switch off the bread machine.

PAIN DE SEIGLE

Based on a rye starter, this is typical of the breads eaten in the Pyrenees. Serve it thickly buttered – it makes the perfect accompaniment for shellfish.

3 Leave the chef to ferment in the machine, with the lid closed, for about 24 hours. If you need the machine, transfer the chef to a bowl, cover it with a damp dishtowel and then set aside at room temperature.

4 Remove the bread pan from the machine. Return the chef to the bread pan, if necessary, and add the water and flour for the first refreshment. Set the bread machine to the dough setting, press Start and mix for 10 minutes. Switch off the machine and leave the dough inside for a further 24 hours.

5 Add the water and flour for the second refreshment. Mix as for the first refreshment, but this time leave the dough in the machine for only 8 hours.

6 Add the water for the bread dough to the mixture in the bread machine pan. Sprinkle in the flour. Place the salt and honey in separate corners of the bread pan. Make a small indent in the centre of the flour and add the yeast. Set the bread machine to the dough setting; use basic dough setting (if available). Press Start. Lightly flour a baking sheet.

COOK'S TIP
When shaping the loaf into a twist make sure that you continue to twist it in the same direction after you have turned the dough round to finish shaping the loaf.

7 When the dough cycle has finished, place the dough on a lightly floured surface. Knock back (punch down) gently, then divide the dough into two equal pieces. Roll each piece of dough into a rope about 45cm/18in long.

8 Place the two ropes side by side. Starting at the centre, place one piece of dough over the other. Continue twisting in this fashion until you reach the end of the rope. Turn the dough around and twist the other ends. Dampen the ends with water; tuck them under to seal.

9 Place the twist on the baking sheet, cover with oiled clear film (plastic wrap) and leave in a warm place for 45 minutes, or until almost doubled in size.

10 Preheat the oven to 220°C/425°F/ Gas 7. Dust the top of the loaf lightly with flour and bake for 40 minutes, or until the bread is golden and sounds hollow when tapped on the base. Switch off the oven, but leave the loaf inside, with the door slightly ajar, for 5 minutes. Turn out on to a wire rack to cool.

SAN FRANCISCO-STYLE SOURDOUGH

This tangy, chewy bread originated in San Francisco, but the flavour will actually be unique to wherever it is baked. The bread is made without baker's yeast, instead using airborne yeast spores to ferment a flour and water paste.

FOR THE STARTER
25g/1oz/¼ cup organic plain (all-purpose) flour
15–30ml/1–2 tbsp warm water

FIRST REFRESHMENT FOR THE STARTER
30ml/2 tbsp water
15ml/1 tbsp milk
50g/2oz/½ cup organic plain (all-purpose) flour

SECOND REFRESHMENT FOR THE STARTER
90ml/6 tbsp water
15–30ml/1–2 tbsp milk
175g/6oz/1½ cups organic strong white flour

FOR THE DOUGH
100ml/3½fl oz/7 tbsp water
175g/6oz/1½ cups organic strong white flour

FIRST REFRESHMENT FOR THE DOUGH
100ml/3½fl oz/7 tbsp water
175g/6oz/1½ cups organic strong white flour
50g/2oz/½ cup organic strong wholemeal (whole-wheat bread) flour
7.5ml/1½ tsp salt
5ml/1 tsp granulated sugar

MAKES 1 LOAF

1 Place the flour in a bowl and stir in enough water for the starter to make a firm, moist dough. Knead for 5 minutes. Cover with a damp cloth. Leave for 2–3 days until a crust forms and the dough inflates with tiny bubbles. Remove the hardened crust and place the moist centre in a clean bowl. Add the water and milk for the first refreshment.

2 Gradually add the flour and mix to a firm but moist dough. Cover and leave for 1–2 days as before. Then repeat as for the first refreshment using the ingredients for the second. Leave for 8–12 hours in a warm place until well risen.

3 Pour the water for the dough into the pan. Add 200g/7oz/scant 1 cup of starter. If necessary for your machine, add the dry ingredients first. Sprinkle in the flour, covering the water. Set the machine to the dough setting; use basic dough setting (if available). Press Start.

4 Mix for 10 minutes then turn off the machine. Leave the dough in the machine for 8 hours. Add the water for the first dough refreshment to the pan, then sprinkle in the flours.

5 Add the salt and sugar in separate corners. Set the machine as before. Press Start. Lightly flour a baking sheet.

6 When the dough cycle ends put the dough on a floured surface. Knock back (punch down) gently; shape into a plump ball. Place on the baking sheet; cover with oiled clear film (plastic wrap). Leave to rise for 2 hours, or until almost doubled in bulk.

7 Preheat the oven to 230°C/450°F/ Gas 8. Dust the loaf with flour and slash the top in a star. Bake for 25 minutes, spraying the oven with water three times in the first 5 minutes. Reduce the oven temperature to 200°C/400°F/Gas 6. Bake for 10 minutes more or until golden and hollow-sounding. Cool on a rack.

CHALLAH

The flavour of this traditional Jewish festival bread is enhanced by the use of a sponge starter, which is left to develop for 8–10 hours before the final dough is made. The dough is often plaited, but can also be shaped into a coil. This shape is favoured for Jewish New Year celebrations, and symbolizes continuity and eternity.

FOR THE SPONGE
200ml/7fl oz/⅞ cup water
225g/8oz/2 cups unbleached strong white (bread) flour
15ml/1 tbsp granulated sugar
5ml/1 tsp salt
7.5ml/1½ tsp easy-blend (rapid-rise) dried yeast

FOR THE DOUGH
2 eggs
225g/8oz/2 cups unbleached strong white flour
15ml/1 tbsp granulated sugar
5ml/1 tsp salt
50g/2oz/¼ cup butter, melted

FOR THE TOPPING
1 egg yolk
15ml/1 tbsp water
poppy seeds

MAKES 1 LOAF

1 Pour the water for the sponge into the bread machine pan. Reverse the order in which you add the wet and dry ingredients if necessary.

2 Sprinkle in the flour making sure that it covers the water. Add the sugar and salt in separate corners. Make an indent in the the flour and add the yeast.

3 Set the bread machine to the dough setting; use basic dough setting (if available). Press Start.

4 When the dough cycle has finished, switch the machine off, leaving the sponge inside. Do not lift the lid. Leave the sponge in the machine for 8 hours. If necessary, transfer to a bowl, cover with a damp dishtowel and set aside.

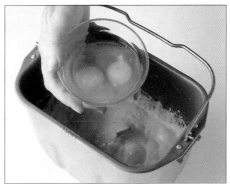

5 Remove the bread pan from the machine and replace the sponge (if necessary). Add the eggs for the dough to the sponge. Sprinkle in the flour. Place the sugar, salt and melted butter in separate corners of the bread pan. Set the bread machine to the dough setting; use basic dough setting (if available). Press Start. Lightly oil a baking sheet.

6 When the dough cycle has finished, remove from the machine and place it on a lightly floured surface. Knock back (punch down) gently, then flatten the dough until it is about 2.5cm/1in thick. Fold both sides to the centre, fold the dough over again and press to seal.

7 Using the palms of your hands, gradually roll the dough into a rope with tapered ends. It should be about 50cm/20in long. Coil the rope into a spiral shape, sealing the final end by tucking it under the loaf. Place the coil on the prepared baking sheet. Cover it with a large glass bowl and leave to rise in a warm place for 45–60 minutes, or until almost doubled in size.

8 Preheat the oven to 190°C/375°F/Gas 5. In a small bowl, beat the egg yolk with the water for the topping. Brush the mixture over the challah. Sprinkle evenly with the poppy seeds and bake for 35–40 minutes, or until the bread is a deep golden brown and sounds hollow when tapped on the base. Transfer it to a wire rack to cool before slicing.

SAVOURY BREADS

—◆—

Adding flavourings, such as herbs and vegetables, provides many new ideas. The subtle

orange hue from pumpkin or carrot, the orange-red crumb from tomatoes and the amazing

colour of spinach bread are only part of the story. Vegetables – grated, puréed, mashed or

chopped – can be incorporated into bread doughs to provide wonderfully flavoured and

coloured loaves. Almost any vegetable can be used, often in conjunction with spices.

SPINACH AND PARMESAN BLOOMER

This pretty pale green loaf is flavoured with spinach, onion and Parmesan cheese. Whole pine nuts are dispersed through the dough of this perfect summertime bread.

15ml/1 tbsp olive oil
1 onion, chopped
115g/4oz fresh young spinach leaves
120ml/generous 4fl oz/½ cup water
1 egg
450g/1lb/4 cups unbleached strong white (bread) flour
2.5ml/½ tsp freshly grated nutmeg
50g/2oz/⅔ cup freshly grated Parmesan cheese
7.5ml/1½ tsp salt
5ml/1 tsp granulated sugar
7.5ml/1½ tsp easy-blend (rapid-rise) dried yeast
30ml/2 tbsp pine nuts

MAKES 1 LOAF

1 Heat the olive oil in a frying pan, add the chopped onion and sauté until a light golden colour. Add the spinach, stir well to combine and cover the pan very tightly. Remove from the heat and leave to stand for 5 minutes. Then stir again and leave the pan uncovered, to cool.

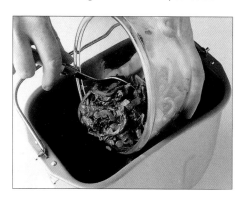

2 Tip the spinach mixture into the bread machine pan. Add the water and egg. If the instructions for your machine specify that the yeast is to be placed in the pan first, then simply reverse the order in which you add the liquid mixture and dry ingredients.

3 Sprinkle over the strong white flour, ensuring that it completely covers the liquid mixture in the bread pan. Sprinkle the grated nutmeg and the Parmesan cheese over the flour.

4 Place the salt and sugar in separate corners of the bread pan. Make a small indent in the centre of the flour, but not down as far as the liquid, and add the easy-blend dried yeast.

5 Set the bread machine to the dough setting; use basic raisin dough setting (if available). Press Start. Lightly flour two baking sheets.

6 Add the pine nuts to the dough when the machine beeps or during the last 5 minutes of the kneading process.

7 When the dough cycle has finished, remove the dough from the machine and place it on a surface that has been lightly floured. Gently knock back (punch down), then carefully roll it out to a rectangle about 2.5cm/1in thick.

8 Roll up the rectangle of dough from one long side to form a thick baton shape, with a square end.

9 Place the baton on the prepared baking sheet, seam side up, cover it with lightly oiled clear film (plastic wrap) and leave to rest for 15 minutes.

10 Turn the bread over and place on the second baking sheet. Plump up the dough by tucking the ends and sides under. Cover it with lightly oiled clear film again and leave it to rise in a warm place for 30 minutes. Meanwhile preheat the oven to 220°C/425°F/Gas 7.

11 Using a sharp knife, slash the top of the bloomer with five diagonal slashes. Bake it for 30–35 minutes, or until it is golden and the bottom sounds hollow when tapped. Turn the bread out on to a wire rack to cool.

VARIATION
Use Swiss chard instead of spinach, if you like. Choose young leaves, stripping them off the ribs. If fresh spinach is unavailable you could replace it with thawed frozen spinach. Make sure any excess water has been squeezed out first, before placing in the bread machine. It may be worth holding a little of the water back and checking the dough as it starts to mix in step 5.

CHILLI BREAD

There's a warm surprise waiting for anyone who bites into this tasty wholemeal bread. Fresh chillies are speckled throughout the crumb. Use Kenyan chillies for a milder flavour or Scotch Bonnets for a fiery taste.

SMALL
15ml/1 tbsp sunflower oil
1–2 fresh chillies, chopped
210ml/7½fl oz/scant 1 cup water
250g/9oz/2¼ cups unbleached strong white (bread) flour
125g/4½oz/generous 1 cup strong wholemeal (whole-wheat bread) flour
7.5ml/1½ tsp salt
7.5ml/1½ tsp granulated sugar
25g/1oz/2 tbsp butter
5ml/1 tsp easy-blend (rapid-rise) dried yeast

MEDIUM
15ml/1 tbsp sunflower oil
2–3 fresh chillies, chopped
320ml/11fl oz/generous 1⅓ cups water
350g/12oz/3 cups unbleached strong white flour
150g/5½oz/1⅓ cups strong wholemeal bread flour
10ml/2 tsp salt
10ml/2 tsp granulated sugar
25g/1oz/2 tbsp butter
5ml/1 tsp easy-blend dried yeast

LARGE
30ml/2 tbsp sunflower oil
3–4 fresh chillies, chopped
420ml/15fl oz/generous 1¾ cups water
475g/1lb 1oz/4¼ cups unbleached strong white flour
200g/7oz/1¾ cups strong wholemeal flour
10ml/2 tsp salt
15ml/1 tbsp granulated sugar
40g/1½oz/3 tbsp butter
7.5ml/1½ tsp easy-blend dried yeast

MAKES 1 LOAF

VARIATION
Use chilli flakes instead of fresh chillies, if you like. You will need 10–20 ml/2–4 tsp, depending on the size of the loaf and how hot you wish to make the bread.

1 Heat the oil in a small frying pan. Add the chillies and sauté them over a moderate heat for 3–4 minutes until softened. Set aside to cool.

2 Tip the chillies and their oil into the bread machine pan. Pour in the water. Reverse the order in which you add the wet and dry ingredients if necessary.

3 Sprinkle in the white and wholemeal flours, making sure that the liquid is covered. Place the salt, sugar and butter in separate corners of the bread machine pan. Make an indent in the flour, but not down as far as the liquid, and add the yeast.

4 Set the bread machine to the basic/normal setting, medium crust. Press Start.

5 Remove the bread at the end of the baking cycle and turn out on to a wire rack to cool.

COURGETTE COUNTRY GRAIN BREAD

The grated courgette combines with the flour during the kneading process to make a succulent bread, while the seeds add both texture and flavour.

1 Pour the buttermilk and water into the bread machine pan. Sprinkle in the grated courgette. If the instructions for your machine specify that the yeast is to be placed in the pan first, reverse the order in which you add the liquid and dry ingredients.

2 Sprinkle in both types of flour, making sure the liquids are completely covered. Add the sunflower seeds, pumpkin seeds and millet seeds. Place the salt, sugar and butter in separate corners of the bread pan. Make a small indent in the flour, but not down as far as the liquid, and add the yeast.

3 Set the bread machine to the basic/normal setting, medium crust. Press Start. Just before the baking cycle, brush the top with water and sprinkle with maize flour.

4 Remove the bread at the end of the baking cycle and turn out on to a wire rack to cool.

SMALL

55ml/2fl oz/¼ cup buttermilk
70ml/2½fl oz/5 tbsp water
115g/4oz/⅔ cup grated
courgettes (zucchini)
280g/10oz/2½ cups unbleached strong
white (bread) flour
50g/2oz/½ cup strong wholemeal
(whole-wheat bread) flour
15ml/1 tbsp sunflower seeds
15ml/1 tbsp pumpkin seeds
5ml/1 tsp millet seeds
5ml/1 tsp salt
5ml/1 tsp granulated sugar
25g/1oz/2 tbsp butter
5ml/1 tsp easy-blend (rapid-rise)
dried yeast
maize flour (cornmeal), for sprinkling

MEDIUM

75ml/5 tbsp buttermilk
55ml/2fl oz/¼ cup water
175g/6oz/1 cup grated courgettes
375g/13oz/3¼ cups unbleached
strong white flour
75g/3oz/¾ cup strong wholemeal flour
22ml/1½ tbsp sunflower seeds
22ml/1½ tbsp pumpkin seeds
10ml/2 tsp millet seeds
7.5ml/1½ tsp salt
7.5ml/1½ tsp granulated sugar
40g/1½oz/3 tbsp butter
7.5ml/1½ tsp easy-blend dried yeast
maize flour, for sprinkling

LARGE

100ml/3½fl oz/7 tbsp buttermilk
130ml/4½fl oz/generous ½ cup water
225g/8oz/1⅓ cups grated courgettes
500g/1lb 2oz/4½ cups unbleached
strong white flour
115g/4oz/1 cup strong wholemeal flour
30ml/2 tbsp sunflower seeds
30ml/2 tbsp pumpkin seeds
15ml/1 tbsp millet seeds
10ml/2 tsp salt
10ml/2 tsp granulated sugar
50g/2oz/¼ cup butter
7.5ml/1½ tsp easy-blend dried yeast
maize flour, for sprinkling

MAKES 1 LOAF

PARSNIP AND NUTMEG BREAD

The moment you cut into this loaf, the irresistible aroma of nutmeg and parsnips fills the air. Stopping at a single slice is the tricky part.

SMALL

225ml/7fl oz/scant 1 cup water
125g/4½oz/1½ cups mashed
cooked parsnips
375g/13oz/3¼ cups unbleached strong
white (bread) flour
15ml/1 tbsp skimmed milk powder
(non fat dry milk)
2.5ml/½ tsp freshly grated nutmeg
25g/1oz/2 tbsp butter
5ml/1 tsp salt
5ml/1 tsp granulated sugar
5ml/1 tsp easy-blend (rapid-rise)
dried yeast

MEDIUM

225ml/8fl oz/scant 1 cup water
175g/6oz/2 cups mashed
cooked parsnips
500g/1lb 2oz/4½ cups unbleached
strong white flour
30ml/2 tbsp skimmed milk powder
5ml/1 tsp freshly grated nutmeg
40g/1½oz/3 tbsp butter
7.5ml/1½ tsp salt
7.5ml/1½ tsp granulated sugar
7.5ml/1½ tsp easy-blend dried yeast

LARGE

320ml/11½fl oz/scant 1½ cups water
225g/8oz/2⅔ cups mashed
cooked parsnips
675g/1½lb/6 cups unbleached
strong white flour
45ml/3 tbsp skimmed milk powder
5ml/1 tsp freshly grated nutmeg
50g/2oz/¼ cup butter
10ml/2 tsp salt
10ml/2 tsp granulated sugar
7.5ml/1½ tsp easy-blend dried yeast

MAKES 1 LOAF

COOK'S TIP

Drain the parsnips thoroughly before mashing so that the dough does not become too wet. Leave the mashed parsnips to cool completely before adding them to the bread.

1 Pour the water into the bread machine pan and add the mashed parsnips. If the instructions for your machine specify that the yeast is to be placed in the pan first, reverse the order in which you add the liquid mixture and dry ingredients.

2 Sprinkle in the flour, making sure it covers the ingredients already placed in the pan. Add the milk powder and freshly grated nutmeg. Place the butter, salt and sugar in separate corners of the bread machine pan. Make a small indent in the centre of the flour, but do not go down as far as the liquid, and add the easy-blend dried yeast.

3 Set the bread machine to the basic/normal setting, medium crust. Press Start.

4 Remove the bread at the end of the baking cycle and turn out on to a wire rack to cool.

BEETROOT BREAD

This spectacular bread takes on the colour of the beetroot juice. It is also flecked with beetroot flesh, which gives the finished loaf a slightly sweet flavour and delightful consistency.

SMALL
150ml/5fl oz/⅔ cup water
140g/5oz/1 cup grated raw beetroot (beet)
2 spring onions (scallions), chopped
375g/13oz/3¼ cups unbleached strong white (bread) flour
15g/½oz/1 tbsp butter
7.5ml/1½ tsp salt
5ml/1 tsp granulated sugar
5ml/1 tsp easy-blend (rapid-rise) dried yeast

MEDIUM
170ml/6fl oz/¾ cup water
225g/8oz/1½ cups grated raw beetroot
3 spring onions, chopped
500g/1lb 2oz/4½ cups unbleached strong white flour
25g/1oz/2 tbsp butter
10ml/2 tsp salt
5ml/1 tsp granulated sugar
5ml/1 tsp easy-blend dried yeast

LARGE
280ml/10fl oz/1¼ cups water
280g/10oz/2 cups grated raw beetroot
4 spring onions, chopped
675g/1½lb/6 cups unbleached strong white (bread) flour
40g/1½oz/3 tbsp butter
10ml/2 tsp salt
7.5ml/1½ tsp granulated sugar
7.5ml/1½ tsp easy-blend dried yeast

MAKES 1 LOAF

3 Sprinkle in the flour over the beetroot and water, making sure it covers them both. Add the butter, salt and sugar in separate corners of the bread pan. Make a small indent in the centre of the flour and add the yeast.

4 Set the bread machine to the basic/normal setting, medium crust. Press Start. If you like, slash the top of the loaf just before the baking cycle starts.

5 Remove the bread at the end of the baking cycle and turn out on to a wire rack to cool.

1 Pour the water into the bread pan. Sprinkle in the grated beetroot. If the instructions for your machine specify that the yeast is to be placed in the pan first, reverse the order in which you add the liquid mixture and dry ingredients.

2 Add the chopped spring onions. However, if your bread machine offers you the option of adding any extra ingredients during the kneading cycle, set the spring onions aside so that you may add them later on.

85ml/3fl oz/³⁄₈ cup milk
120ml/4fl oz/½ cup water
1 egg
400g/14oz/3½ cups unbleached strong
white (bread) flour
100g/3½oz/scant 1 cup yellow
cornmeal
5ml/1 tsp granulated sugar
5ml/1 tsp salt
7.5ml/1½ tsp easy-blend (rapid-rise)
dried yeast
15ml/1 tbsp chopped fresh green chilli
115g/4oz/⅔ cup drained canned
sweetcorn kernels
25g/1oz/2 tbsp butter

MAKES 1 LOAF

1 Pour the milk and water into the bread pan. Add the egg. Reverse the order in which you add the liquid and dry ingredients, if necessary. Sprinkle in the flour and cornmeal, covering the liquid. Add the sugar and salt in separate corners. Make a small indent in the flour; add the yeast.

BUBBLE CORN BREAD

——

This recipe brings together two traditional American breads – corn bread and bubble loaf. It has the flavour of corn and is spiked with hot chilli. Chunks or "bubbles" of bread can easily be pulled from the bread for easy eating.

2 Set the bread machine to the dough setting; use basic raisin dough setting (if available). Press Start. Add the chilli and sweetcorn when the machine beeps or during the last 5 minutes of kneading. Lightly oil a baking sheet.

3 When the dough cycle has finished, remove the dough and gently knock back (punch down), then cut it into 20 equal pieces. Shape into balls.

4 Arrange half of the dough balls in the base of a 22cm/8½in non-stick springform cake tin (pan), spacing them slightly apart. Place the remaining balls of dough on top of the first layer so that they cover the spaces.

5 Cover the tin with oiled clear film (plastic wrap) and leave to rise in a warm place for about 30–45 minutes, or until the dough has almost doubled in bulk. Meanwhile, preheat the oven to 200°C/400°F/Gas 6.

6 Melt the butter in a small pan. Drizzle it over the top of the risen loaf. Bake the bread for 30–35 minutes, or until golden and well risen. Turn the bread out on to a wire rack to cool. Serve warm or cold.

½ red (bell) pepper, seeded
½ green (bell) pepper, seeded
½ yellow (bell) pepper, seeded
200ml/7fl oz/⅞ cup milk
120ml/generous 4fl oz/½ cup water
500g/1lb 2oz/4½ cups unbleached
strong white (bread) flour
10ml/2 tsp granulated sugar
7.5ml/1½ tsp salt
7.5ml/1½ tsp easy-blend (rapid-rise)
dried yeast
milk, for brushing
5ml/1 tsp cumin seeds

MAKES 1 LOAF

1 Cut the peppers into fine dice. Pour the milk and water into the bread pan. Reverse the order in which you add the wet and dry ingredients if necessary.

2 Sprinkle in the flour, making sure that it covers the liquid. Add the sugar and salt in separate corners of the pan.

MIXED PEPPER BREAD

——

Colourful and full of flavour, this bread looks good when sliced, as the pretty pepper studs can be seen to advantage. Add orange pepper too, if you like.

3 Make a small indent in the centre of the flour and add the yeast. Set the bread machine to the dough setting; use basic raisin dough setting (if available). Press Start. Lightly oil a baking sheet.

4 Add the mixed peppers when the machine beeps or during the last 5 minutes of kneading.

5 When the dough cycle has finished, transfer the dough to a lightly floured surface. Gently knock back (punch down) and shape it into a round, plump ball. Roll gently into an oval. Place on the prepared baking sheet, cover with oiled clear film (plastic wrap) and leave to rise for 30–45 minutes, or until doubled in bulk.

6 Preheat the oven to 200°C/400°F/Gas 6. Brush the loaf top with the milk and sprinkle with the cumin seeds. Use a sharp knife to cut a lengthways slash.

7 Bake for 35–40 minutes, or until the bread is golden and the bottom sounds hollow when tapped. Turn the bread out on to a wire rack to cool.

SUN-DRIED TOMATO AND CEP LOAF

The powerful concentrated flavours of cep mushrooms and sun-dried tomatoes exude from this Mediterranean-style bread.

SMALL
10g/⅓oz dried cep
(porcini) mushrooms
200ml/7fl oz/⅞ cup warm water
375g/13oz/3¼ cups unbleached strong
white (bread) flour
7.5ml/1½ tsp salt
15ml/1 tbsp granulated sugar
25g/1oz/2 tbsp butter
5ml/1 tsp easy-blend (rapid-rise)
dried yeast
25g/1oz/¼ cup well-drained
sun-dried tomatoes in olive oil

MEDIUM
15g/½oz dried cep mushrooms
200ml/7fl oz/⅞ cup
warm water
500g/1lb 2oz/4½ cups unbleached
strong white flour
7.5ml/1½ tsp salt
15ml/1 tbsp granulated sugar
25g/1oz/2 tbsp butter
5ml/1 tsp easy-blend dried yeast
40g/1½oz/⅓ cup well-drained
sun-dried tomatoes in olive oil

LARGE
25g/1oz dried cep mushrooms
200ml/7fl oz/⅞ cup warm water
675g/1½lb/6 cups unbleached
strong white flour
10ml/2 tsp salt
22ml/1½ tbsp granulated sugar
40g/1½oz/3 tbsp butter
7.5ml/1½ tsp easy-blend dried yeast
50g/2oz/½ cup well-drained
sun-dried tomatoes in olive oil

MAKES 1 LOAF

1 Place the dried mushrooms in a small bowl and pour over the warm water. Leave to soak for 30 minutes. Pour the mushrooms into a strainer placed over a bowl. Drain thoroughly, reserving the soaking liquid. Set the mushrooms aside. Make up the soaking liquid to 210ml/7½fl oz/scant 1 cup, 320ml/11fl oz/generous 1⅓ cups or 420ml/15fl oz/generous 1⅔ cups, depending on the size of loaf you are making.

2 Pour the liquid into the bread pan. If necessary, reverse the order in which you add the liquid and dry ingredients.

3 Sprinkle in the flour, covering the water. Add the salt, sugar and butter, placing them in separate corners.

COOK'S TIP
Add a tablespoon or two of extra flour if the dough is too soft after adding the mushrooms and tomatoes.

4 Make a small indent in the flour; add the yeast. Set the bread machine to the basic/normal setting; use raisin setting (if available), medium crust. Press Start.

5 Chop the reserved mushrooms and the tomatoes. Add them to the dough when the machine beeps, or during the last 5 minutes of the kneading cycle.

6 Remove the bread at the end of the baking cycle and turn out on to a wire rack to cool.

CARROT AND FENNEL BREAD

The distinctive flavour of fennel is the perfect foil for the more subtle carrot taste in this unusual bread. It looks pretty when sliced, thanks to the attractive orange flecks of carrot.

SMALL
180ml/6½fl oz/generous ¾ cup water
15ml/1 tbsp sunflower oil
5ml/1 tsp clear honey
140g/5oz/1 cup grated carrot
375g/13oz/3¼ cups unbleached strong
white (bread) flour
15ml/1 tbsp skimmed milk powder
(non fat dry milk)
5ml/1 tsp fennel seeds
5ml/1 tsp salt
5ml/1 tsp easy-blend (rapid-rise)
dried yeast

MEDIUM
210ml/7½fl oz/scant 1 cup water
30ml/2 tbsp sunflower oil
10ml/2 tsp clear honey
200g/7oz/scant 1½ cups grated carrot
500g/1lb 2oz/4½ cups unbleached
strong white flour
30ml/2 tbsp skimmed milk powder
7.5ml/1½ tsp fennel seeds
7.5ml/1½ tsp salt
5ml/1 tsp easy-blend dried yeast

LARGE
285ml/10fl oz/1¼ cups water
45ml/3 tbsp sunflower oil
15ml/1 tbsp clear honey
250g/9oz/scant 2 cups grated carrot
675g/1½lb/6 cups unbleached
strong white flour
45ml/3 tbsp skimmed milk powder
10ml/2 tsp fennel seeds
10ml/2 tsp salt
7.5ml/1½ tsp easy-blend dried yeast

MAKES 1 LOAF

3 Set the machine to the basic/normal setting, medium crust. Press Start.

4 Remove the bread at the end of the baking cycle and cook on to a wire rack.

COOK'S TIP
When adding the grated carrot, sprinkle it in lightly and evenly. This avoids clumps, which would not mix evenly through the dough.

1 Pour the water, oil and honey into the bread machine pan. Sprinkle in the grated carrot. If the instructions for your machine specify that the yeast is to be placed in the pan first, reverse the order in which you add the liquid and dry ingredients.

2 Sprinkle in the flour, making sure that it covers the water. Add the milk powder and fennel seeds. Add the salt in one corner of the bread pan. Make a small indent in the centre of the flour, but not down as far as the liquid, and add the yeast.

210ml/7½fl oz/scant 1 cup water
350g/12oz/3 cups unbleached strong
white (bread) flour
25g/1oz/¼ cup wholemeal
(whole-wheat) bread flour
15ml/1 tbsp skimmed milk powder
(non fat dry milk)
5ml/1 tsp salt
7.5ml/1½ tsp granulated sugar
5ml/1 tsp easy-blend (rapid-rise)
dried yeast
40g/1½oz/scant ½ cup well drained,
pitted black olives, chopped
50g/2oz feta cheese, crumbled
15ml/1 tbsp olive oil, for brushing

MAKES 1 LOAF

COOK'S TIP
Depending on the moisture content of
the olives and cheese you may need
to add a tablespoon or two of flour to
the bread dough when adding them.

FETA CHEESE AND BLACK OLIVE LOAF

*Conjuring up memories of holidays in Greece, this bread has a delicious
flavour, thanks to the Mediterranean ingredients.*

1 Pour the water into the bread pan. If
necessary, reverse the order in which
you add the liquid and dry ingredients.
Sprinkle in the flours, covering the
water completely. Add the skimmed
milk powder. Place the salt and sugar in
separate corners of the bread pan. Make
an indent in the flour; add the yeast.

2 Set the bread machine to the dough
setting; use basic raisin dough setting
(if available). Press Start. Lightly oil an
18–20cm/7–8in deep round cake tin (pan).

3 Add the olives and feta when the
bread machine beeps or 5 minutes
before the end of the kneading cycle.
Once the dough cycle has finished, place
the dough on a lightly floured surface
and knock back (punch down) gently.

4 Shape the dough into a plump ball, the
diameter of the tin. Place in the tin,
cover with oiled clear film (plastic wrap)
and leave to rise for 30–45 minutes.
Preheat the oven to 200°C/400°F/Gas 6.

5 Remove the clear film and brush the
olive oil over the top of the loaf. Bake
for 35–40 minutes, or until golden. Turn
the bread out on to a wire rack to cool.

LEEK AND PANCETTA TRAY BREAD

*What could be more delicious than this rich yeast dough, topped with leeks
and pancetta in a sour cream custard? Serve it sliced, with a simple salad
of dressed leaves, for a tasty supper or lunchtime snack.*

90ml/6 tbsp water
1 egg
225g/8oz/2 cups unbleached strong
white (bread) flour
5ml/1 tsp salt
25g/1oz butter
5ml/1 tsp easy-blend (rapid-rise)
dried yeast

FOR THE FILLING
575g/1¼lb/4–5 leeks
30ml/2 tbsp sunflower oil
75g/3oz sliced pancetta or streaky
(fatty) bacon, cut into strips
140ml/5fl oz/⅝ cup sour cream
70ml/2½fl oz/5 tbsp milk
2 eggs, lightly beaten
15ml/1 tbsp chopped fresh basil leaves
salt and freshly ground black pepper

MAKES 1 LOAF

1 Pour the water and egg into the pan.
If necessary, reverse the order in which
you add the liquid and dry ingredients.

2 Sprinkle in the flour, making sure that
it covers the water and egg. Place the
salt and butter in separate corners of
the bread pan. Make a shallow indent
in the centre of the flour, but not down
as far as the liquid, and add the easy-
blend dried yeast.

3 Set the bread machine to the dough
setting; use basic or pizza dough setting
(if available). Press Start. Then lightly
oil a 20 x 30cm/8 x 12in Swiss (jelly) roll
tin (pan) that is about 1cm/½in deep.

4 Slice the leeks thinly. Heat the
sunflower oil in a large frying pan and
cook the leeks over a low heat for about
5 minutes, until they have softened
slightly but not browned. Set them
aside to cool.

5 When the dough cycle has finished,
place the dough on a lightly floured
surface. Knock back (punch down)
gently, then roll it out to a 23 x 33 cm/
9 x 13in rectangle. Place in the prepared
tin and press the edges outwards and
upwards, so that the dough covers the
base and sides evenly. Preheat the oven
to 190°C/375°F/Gas 5.

6 Sprinkle the leeks over the dough.
Arrange the pancetta slices on top.
Mix the sour cream, milk and eggs
together. Add the basil and season with
salt and ground black pepper. Pour the
mixture over the leeks.

7 Bake for 30–35 minutes, or until the
filling has set and the base is golden
around the edges. Serve hot or warm.

FRESH TOMATO AND BASIL LOAF

Here are some classic Mediterranean flavours incorporated into a bread. Sweet plum tomatoes, onions and fresh basil complement each other in this attractively shaped loaf. Serve to accompany lunch either with butter or with individual bowls of best quality extra virgin olive oil for dipping.

15ml/1 tbsp extra virgin olive oil
1 small onion, chopped
3 plum tomatoes, about 200g/7oz, peeled, seeded and chopped
500g/1lb 2oz/4½ cups unbleached strong white (bread) flour
2.5ml/½ tsp freshly ground black pepper
7.5ml/1½ tsp salt
10ml/2 tsp granulated sugar
5ml/1 tsp easy-blend (rapid-rise) dried yeast
15ml/1 tbsp chopped fresh basil

FOR THE GLAZE
1 egg yolk
15ml/1 tbsp water

MAKES 1 LOAF

1 Heat the extra virgin olive oil in a pan or small frying pan. Add the chopped onion and cook over a moderate heat, stirring occasionally, for 3–4 minutes, until the onion is softened and light golden in colour.

2 Add the plum tomatoes and cook for 2–3 minutes, until slightly softened. Drain through a strainer placed over a measuring jug (cup) or bowl, pressing the mixture gently with the back of a spoon to extract the juices.

3 Set the tomato and onion mixture aside. Make the cooking juices up to 280ml/10fl oz/1¼ cups with water, but see Variation. Set aside to cool. When the liquid is cold, pour it into the bread machine pan. If the instructions for your machine specify that the yeast is to be placed in the pan first, reverse the order in which you add the liquid and dry ingredients.

4 Sprinkle in the flour, making sure that it covers the tomato and onion liquid. Add the ground black pepper, then place the salt and sugar in separate corners of the bread machine pan.

5 Make a small indent in the centre of the flour, but not down as far as the liquid, and add the yeast.

6 Set the bread machine to the dough setting; use basic dough setting (if available). Press Start. Then lightly oil a 23 x 13cm/9 x 5in loaf tin (pan).

7 When the dough cycle has finished, remove the dough from the machine and place it on a lightly floured surface. Knock back (punch down) gently.

8 Knead in the reserved tomato and onion mixture and the chopped fresh basil. You may need to add a little extra flour if the dough becomes too moist when you have incorporated the vegetable mixture.

9 Flatten the dough and shape it into a 2.5cm/1in thick rectangle. Fold the sides to the middle and press down the edge to seal. Make a hollow along the centre and fold in half again. Gently roll it into a loaf about 40cm/16in long.

10 Shape into an "S" shape and place in the prepared tin. Cover with oiled clear film (plastic wrap) and leave in a warm place for 30–45 minutes. Meanwhile preheat the oven to 200°C/400°F/Gas 6.

11 Make the glaze by mixing the egg yolk and water together. Remove the clear film and brush the glaze over the bread. Bake in the preheated oven for 35–40 minutes, or until golden.

VARIATION
To intensify the tomato flavour of the loaf, substitute 15ml/1 tbsp sun-dried tomato purée (paste) for 15ml/1 tbsp of water when you are topping up the cooking juices in step 3.

POTATO AND SAFFRON BREAD

A dough that includes potato produces a moist loaf with a springy texture and good keeping qualities. Saffron adds an aromatic flavour and rich golden colour to this bread.

1 large potato, about 225g/8oz, peeled
5ml/1 tsp saffron threads
1 egg
450g/1lb/4 cups unbleached strong white (bread) flour
30ml/2 tbsp skimmed milk powder (non fat dry milk)
25g/1oz/2 tbsp butter
15ml/1 tbsp clear honey
7.5ml/1½ tsp salt
7.5ml/1½ tsp easy-blend (rapid-rise) dried yeast

MAKES 1 LOAF

COOK'S TIP
If you have time, soak the saffron for 3–4 hours for a better flavour.

1 Place the potato in a pan of boiling water, reduce the heat and simmer until tender. Drain the potato, reserving 200ml/7fl oz/⅞ cup of the cooking water in a jug (cup). Add the saffron threads to the hot water; leave to stand for 30 minutes. Mash the potato (without adding butter or milk) and leave to cool.

2 Add the saffron water to the bread pan. Add the mashed potato and the egg. Reverse the order in which you add the wet and dry ingredients if necessary.

3 Sprinkle in the flour, making sure that it covers the ingredients already placed in the pan. Spoon in the milk powder. Add the butter, honey and salt in separate corners of the bread pan. Make a small indent in the centre of the flour, but not down as far as the liquid, and add the yeast.

4 Set the bread machine to the dough setting; use basic dough setting (if available). Press Start. Lightly flour a baking sheet.

5 When the dough cycle has finished, remove the dough from the machine and place on a lightly floured surface. Gently knock back (punch down).

6 Shape the dough into a plump ball. Place on the baking sheet, cover with oiled clear film (plastic wrap) and leave to rise for 30–45 minutes. Meanwhile preheat the oven to 200°C/400°F/Gas 6.

7 Slash the top of the loaf with three or four diagonal cuts, then rotate and repeat to make a criss-cross effect.

8 Bake the bread for 35–40 minutes, or until the bottom sounds hollow when tapped. Turn out on to a wire rack.

CARAMELIZED ONION BREAD

The unmistakable, mouthwatering flavour of golden fried onions is captured in this coburg-shaped bread. Serve with soup, cheeses or salad.

50g/2oz/¼ cup butter
2 onions, chopped
280ml/10fl oz/1¼ cups water
15ml/1 tbsp clear honey
450g/1lb/4 cups unbleached strong white (bread) flour
7.5ml/1½ tsp salt
2.5ml/½ tsp freshly ground black pepper
7.5ml/1½ tsp easy-blend (rapid-rise) dried yeast

MAKES 1 LOAF

1 Melt the butter in a frying pan and sauté the onions over a low heat until golden. Remove the pan from the heat and let the onions cool slightly. Place a strainer over the bread machine pan, then tip the contents of the frying pan into it, so that the juices fall into the pan. Set the onions aside to cool.

2 Add the water and honey to the bread pan. Reverse the order in which you add the wet and dry ingredients if necessary. Sprinkle in the flour, covering the liquid. Place the salt and pepper in separate corners. Make a shallow indent in the centre of the flour; add the yeast.

3 Set the bread machine to the dough setting; use basic raisin dough setting (if available). Press Start. Add the onions when the machine beeps or in the last 5 minutes of kneading. Lightly flour a baking sheet.

4 When the cycle has finished, remove the dough from the bread pan and place on a lightly floured surface.

5 Knock back (punch down); shape into a ball. Place on the baking sheet and cover with oiled clear film (plastic wrap). Leave to rise for 45 minutes. Preheat the oven to 200°C/400°F/Gas 6. Slash cross in the top of the loaf. Bake for 35–40 minutes. Cool on a wire rack.

CAJUN SPICED PLAIT

The traditional Deep South flavours of tomatoes, garlic, spices and hot seasonings make this piquant, spicy loaf irresistible.

300ml/10½fl oz/1¼ cups water
30ml/2 tbsp vegetable oil
15ml/1 tbsp tomato purée (paste)
500g/1lb 2oz/4½ cups unbleached strong white (bread) flour
7.5ml/1½ tsp paprika
5ml/1 tsp cayenne pepper
5ml/1 tsp dried oregano
2.5ml/½ tsp freshly ground black pepper
1 garlic clove, crushed
7.5ml/1½ tsp salt
2.5ml/½ tsp sugar
7.5ml/1½ tsp easy-blend (rapid-rise) dried yeast

FOR THE GLAZE
1 egg yolk
15ml/1 tbsp water

MAKES 1 LOAF

1 Pour the water and vegetable oil into the bread machine pan, then add the tomato purée. If the instructions for your machine specify that the yeast is to be placed in the pan first, reverse the order in which you add the liquid and dry ingredients.

2 Sprinkle in the flour, making sure that it covers the liquid. Add the paprika, cayenne, oregano, black pepper and crushed garlic. Place the salt and sugar in separate corners of the bread pan. Make a small indent in the centre of the flour, but not down as far as the liquid and add the yeast.

3 Set the bread machine to the dough setting; use basic dough setting (if available). Press Start. Lightly oil a baking sheet.

4 Once the dough cycle has finished, remove the dough from the machine and place it on a floured surface. Knock back (punch down) and divide into three. Roll the pieces into ropes, all the same length. Put them next to each other. From the centre, plait (braid) from left to right, working towards yourself. Press the ends together and tuck under.

5 Turn the dough around and plait the remaining ropes, as before. Place on the prepared baking sheet, cover with oiled clear film (plastic wrap) and leave in a warm place for 30–45 minutes. Preheat the oven to 200°C/400°F/Gas 6.

6 Mix the egg yolk and water for the glaze together. Remove the clear film and brush the glaze over the plait. Bake for 30–35 minutes, or until golden.

SALAMI AND PEPPERCORN BREAD

This loaf marbled with salami and black pepper makes a great accompaniment to hot soup. For a quick snack, try it toasted with a cheese topping.

210ml/7½fl oz/scant 1 cup water
15ml/1 tbsp olive oil
350g/12oz/3 cups unbleached white flour
50g/2oz/½ cup grated mature (sharp) Cheddar cheese
2.5ml/½ tsp salt
5ml/1 tsp granulated sugar
5ml/1 tsp easy-blend (rapid-rise) dried yeast
5ml/1 tsp black peppercorns, coarsely crushed
50g/2oz salami, chopped
milk, for brushing

MAKES 1 LOAF

1 Pour the water and olive oil into the bread machine pan. If the instructions for your bread machine specify that the easy-blend dried yeast is to be placed in the pan first, then simply reverse the order in which you add the liquid and dry ingredients.

2 Sprinkle in the flour, making sure that it covers the liquid. Add half the cheese. Add the salt in one corner of the bread pan and the sugar in another corner. Make a small indent in the centre of the flour, but not down as far as the liquid, and add the yeast.

3 Set the bread machine to the dough setting; use basic or pizza dough setting (if available). Press Start. Then lightly oil a baking sheet.

4 Once the dough cycle has finished, remove the dough from the machine and place it on a lightly floured surface. Knock back (punch down) gently and flatten it slightly. Sprinkle over the peppercorns and salami and knead gently until both are incorporated.

5 Shape into a round loaf; place on the baking sheet. Cover with an oiled bowl and leave in a warm place for 30 minutes. Preheat the oven to 200°C/400°F/Gas 6.

6 Uncover the bread, brush it with milk and sprinkle with the remaining cheese. Bake for about 30–35 minutes, or until golden. Turn out on to a wire rack to cool.

MARBLED PESTO BREAD

140ml/5fl oz/⅔ cup milk
150ml/5fl oz/scant ⅔ cup water
30ml/2 tbsp extra virgin olive oil
450g/1lb/4 cups unbleached strong
white (bread) flour
7.5ml/1½ tsp granulated sugar
7.5ml/1½ tsp salt
7.5ml/1½ tsp easy-blend (rapid-rise)
dried yeast
100g/3½oz/7 tbsp ready-made
pesto sauce

FOR THE TOPPING
15ml/1 tbsp extra virgin olive oil
10ml/2 tsp coarse sea salt

MAKES 1 LOAF

Using ready-made pesto sauce means that this scrumptious bread is very easy to make. Use a good quality sauce – or, if you have the time, make your own – so that the flavours of garlic, basil, pine nuts and Parmesan cheese can be clearly discerned.

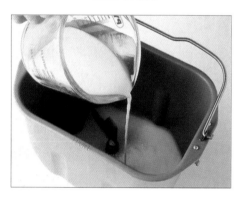

1 Remove the milk from the refrigerator 30 minutes before using, to bring it to room temperature. Pour the water, milk and extra virgin olive oil into the bread machine pan. If the instructions for your bread machine specify that the yeast is to be placed in the pan first, then simply reverse the order in which you add the liquid and dry ingredients.

2 Sprinkle in the flour, making sure that it covers the liquid mixture completely. Add the sugar and salt, placing them in separate corners of the bread pan.

3 Make a small indent in the centre of the flour, but do not go down as far as the liquid, and pour the dried yeast into the hollow.

4 Set the bread machine to the dough setting. If your machine has a choice of settings use the basic dough setting. Press Start. Lightly oil a 25 x 10cm/ 10 x 4in loaf tin (pan).

5 When the dough cycle has finished, remove the dough from the machine and place it on a lightly floured surface.

6 Knock back (punch down) gently. Roll it out to a 2cm/¾in thick rectangle 25cm/10in long. Cover with oiled clear film (plastic wrap) and leave to relax for a few minutes.

7 Spread the pesto sauce over the dough. Leave a clear border of 1cm/½in along one long edge. Roll up the dough lengthways, Swiss (jelly) roll fashion, tuck the ends under and place, seam down, in the prepared tin.

8 Cover with oiled clear film and set aside in a warm place to rise for 45 minutes or until the dough has more than doubled in size and reaches the top of the loaf tin. Meanwhile, preheat the oven to 220°C/425°F/Gas 7.

9 Remove the clear film and brush the olive oil over the top of the loaf. Use a sharp knife to score the top with four diagonal cuts. Repeat the cuts in the opposite direction to make a criss-cross pattern. Sprinkle with the sea salt.

10 Bake for 25–30 minutes, or until the bread is golden and sounds hollow when tapped on the base. Turn out on to a wire rack to cool.

COOK'S TIP

For a really luxurious twist to this bread, make your own pesto filling. Put 75g/3oz/3 cups basil leaves, 1 garlic clove, 30ml/2 tbsp pine nuts, salt and pepper, and 90ml/6 tbsp olive oil in a mortar and crush to a paste with a pestle, or alternatively, place in a blender and blend until creamy. Work in 50g/2oz/⅔ cup freshly grated Parmesan cheese. Any leftover pesto can be kept for up to 2 weeks in the refrigerator.

1 egg
100ml/3½ fl oz/7 tbsp milk
225g/8oz/2 cups unbleached strong
white (bread) flour
5ml/1 tsp salt
2.5ml/½ tsp caster (superfine) sugar
50g/2oz/¼ cup butter
5ml/1 tsp easy-blend (rapid-rise)
dried yeast
30ml/2 tbsp milk,
for glazing (optional)

MAKES 12 ROLLS

COOK'S TIP
Make double the quantity and freeze the surplus. You will need only the same amount of yeast.

1 Pour the egg and milk into the bread pan. If necessary for your machine, place the dry ingredients in the pan before the liquid.

BRIDGE ROLLS
———

Milk and egg flavour these small, soft-textured finger rolls. Use them for canapés or serve them with soup.

2 Sprinkle in the flour, making sure that it covers the liquid. Add the salt, sugar and butter, placing them in separate corners of the bread machine pan. Then make a small indent in the centre of the flour, but do not go down as far as the liquid, and add the easy-blend dried yeast.

3 Set the bread machine to the dough setting; use basic dough setting (if available). Press Start. Lightly oil two baking sheets.

4 When the dough cycle has finished, remove the dough from the bread machine and place it on a lightly floured surface. Knock back (punch down) gently, then divide into 12 pieces and cover with a piece of oiled clear film (plastic wrap).

5 Take one piece of dough, leaving the rest covered, and shape it on the floured surface into a tapered long roll. Repeat with the remaining dough until you have 12 evenly shaped rolls.

6 Place six rolls in a row, keeping them fairly close to each other, on each baking sheet. Cover with oiled clear film and leave in a warm place for about 30 minutes, or until the rolls have doubled in size and are touching each other. Meanwhile, preheat the oven to 220°C/425°F/Gas 7.

7 Brush the bridge rolls with milk, if you like, and bake them for 15–18 minutes, or until lightly browned. Transfer the batch to a wire rack to cool, then separate into rolls.

140ml/5fl oz/scant ⅔ cup milk
140ml/5fl oz/scant ⅔ cup water
225g/8oz/2 cups strong stoneground
wholemeal (whole-wheat bread) flour,
plus extra for dusting
225g/8oz/2 cups unbleached strong
white (bread) flour
7.5ml/1½ tsp salt
10ml/2 tsp caster (superfine) sugar
5ml/1 tsp easy-blend (rapid-rise)
dried yeast
milk, for glazing

MAKES 10 ROLLS

1 Pour the milk and water into the pan. Reverse the order in which you add the wet and dry ingredients if necessary.

2 Sprinkle in the flours, covering the liquid. Add the salt and sugar in separate corners. Make a shallow indent in the centre of the flour and add the yeast. Set the bread machine to the dough setting; use basic dough setting (if available). Press Start.

BREAKFAST BAPS
———

There's nothing nicer than waking up to the aroma of fresh baked bread. The wholemeal flour adds extra flavour to these soft breakfast rolls.

3 When the dough cycle has finished, remove the dough from the machine and place it on a lightly floured surface. Knock back (punch down) gently, then divide it into ten pieces and cover with lightly oiled clear film (plastic wrap).

4 Take one piece of dough, leaving the rest covered, and cup your hands around it to shape it into a ball. Place it on the lightly floured surface and roll it into a flat oval measuring 10 x 7.5cm/4 x 3in.

5 Repeat with the remaining dough so that you have ten flat oval dough pieces. Lightly oil two baking sheets.

6 Place the baps on the prepared baking sheets. Cover with oiled clear film and leave to rise in a warm place for about 30 minutes, or until the baps are almost doubled in size. Meanwhile, preheat the oven to 200°C/400°F/Gas 6.

7 Using three middle fingers, press each bap in the centre to help disperse any large air bubbles. Brush with milk and dust lightly with wholemeal flour.

8 Bake for 15–20 minutes, or until the baps are lightly browned. Turn out on to a wire rack and serve warm.

50g/2oz/¼ cup butter
1 large onion, finely chopped
280ml/10fl oz/1¼ cups water
280g/10oz/2½ cups unbleached strong
white (bread) flour
115g/4oz/1 cup Granary
(multi-grain) flour
25g/1oz/¼ cup oat bran
10ml/2 tsp salt
10ml/2 tsp clear honey
7.5ml/1½ tsp easy-blend (rapid-rise)
dried yeast
maize flour (cornmeal), for dusting
30ml/2 tbsp millet grain
15ml/1 tbsp coarse oatmeal
15ml/1 tbsp sunflower seeds

MAKES 12 ROLLS

1 Melt half the butter in a frying pan. Add the chopped onions and sauté for 8–10 minutes, or until softened and lightly browned. Set aside to cool.

2 Pour the water into the machine pan. If the instructions for your machine state the yeast is to be placed in the pan first, reverse the order in which you add the wet and dry ingredients.

3 Sprinkle in the strong white flour, Granary flour and oat bran, making sure that the water is completely covered. Add the salt, honey and remaining butter, placing them in separate corners of the bread pan. Make a small indent in the centre of the flour, but not down as far as the liquid, and add the yeast.

4 Set the bread machine to the dough setting; use basic raisin dough setting (if available). Press Start. Lightly oil two baking sheets and sprinkle them with maize flour.

MIXED GRAIN ONION ROLLS

These crunchy rolls, flavoured with golden onions, are perfect for snacks and sandwiches or to serve with soup.

5 Add the millet grain, coarse oatmeal, sunflower seeds and cooked onion when the machine beeps. If your machine does not have this facility add these ingredients 5 minutes before the end of the kneading cycle.

6 When the dough cycle has finished, remove the dough from the bread machine and place it on a surface that has been lightly floured. Knock back (punch down) gently, then divide it into 12 equal pieces.

VARIATION
If time is short you can omit the cutting in step 9 and cook as round shaped rolls.

7 Shape each piece into a ball, making sure that that tops are smooth. Flatten them slightly with the palm of your hand or a small rolling pin. Place the rolls on the prepared baking sheets and dust them with more maize flour.

8 Cover the rolls with oiled clear film (plastic wrap) and leave them in a warm place for 30–45 minutes, or until doubled in size. Meanwhile, preheat the oven to 200°C/400°F/Gas 6.

9 Using a pair of lightly floured sharp scissors snip each roll in five places, cutting inwards from the edge, almost to the centre. Bake for 18–20 minutes, or until the rolls are golden. Turn them out on to a wire rack to cool.

ITALIAN BREADSTICKS

These crisp breadsticks will keep for a couple of days if stored in an airtight container. If you like, you can refresh them in a hot oven for a few minutes before serving. The dough can be made in any bread machine, regardless of capacity.

200ml/7fl oz/⅞ cup water
45ml/3 tbsp olive oil, plus extra
for brushing
350g/12oz/3 cups unbleached strong
white (bread) flour
7.5ml/1½ tsp salt
7.5ml/1½ tsp easy-blend (rapid-rise)
dried yeast
poppy seeds and coarse sea salt,
for coating (optional)

MAKES 30 BREADSTICKS

1 Pour the water and olive oil into the bread machine pan. If the instructions for your machine specify that the yeast is to be placed in the pan first, reverse the order in which you add the liquid and dry ingredients.

2 Sprinkle on the flour, making sure that it covers the water completely. Add the salt in one corner of the pan. Make a small indent in the centre of the flour, but not down as far as the liquid, and add the easy-blend dried yeast.

3 Set the bread machine to the dough setting; use basic dough setting (if available). Press Start.

4 Lightly oil two baking sheets. Preheat the oven to 200°C/400°F/Gas 6.

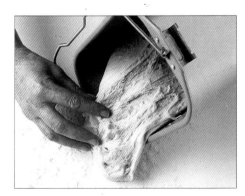

5 When the dough cycle has finished, remove the dough from the machine, place it on a lightly floured surface and knock back (punch down). Roll it out to a 23 x 20cm/9 x 8in rectangle.

6 Cut into three 20cm/8in long strips. Cut each strip widthways into ten. Roll and stretch each piece to 30cm/12in.

7 Roll the breadsticks in poppy seeds or sea salt if liked. Space well apart on the baking sheets. Brush with olive oil, cover with clear film (plastic wrap) and leave in a warm place for 10–15 minutes.

8 Bake for 15–20 minutes, or until golden, turning once. Transfer to a wire rack to cool.

COOK'S TIP
If you are rolling the breadsticks in sea salt, don't use too much or it can overpower the taste. Crush the sea salt slightly if the crystals are large.

200ml/7fl oz/⅞ cup water
45ml/3 tbsp extra virgin olive oil
350g/12½oz/3 cups unbleached strong
white (bread) flour
5ml/1 tsp salt
2.5ml/½ tsp granulated sugar
5ml/1 tsp easy-blend (rapid-rise)
dried yeast

FOR THE TOPPING
30ml/2 tbsp water
15ml/1 tbsp sea salt
15ml/1 tbsp sesame seeds

MAKES ABOUT 70 ROLLS

COOK'S TIP
Make these tasty nibbles up to a day
in advance. Re-heat in a moderate
oven for a few minutes, to refresh.

1 Pour the water and oil into the pan.
If necessary, reverse the order in which
you add the liquid and dry ingredients.

SPANISH PICOS

*These small bread shapes, dusted with salt and sesame seeds, are often eaten
in Spain with pre-dinner drinks, but can also be served as an
accompaniment to an appetizer or soup.*

2 Sprinkle in the flour, making sure that
it covers the liquid. Add the salt and
sugar, placing them in separate corners
of the bread pan. Make a small indent in
the centre of the flour, but not down as
far as the liquid, and add the yeast.

3 Set the machine to the dough setting;
use basic dough setting (if available).
Press Start. Then lightly oil two
baking sheets.

4 When the dough cycle has finished,
remove the dough from the machine
and place it on a lightly floured surface.
Knock back (punch down) gently, then
roll it out to a rectangle measuring
30 x 23cm/12 x 9in. Cut lengthways into
three strips, then cut each strip of
dough into 2.5cm/1in wide ribbons.

5 Preheat the oven to 200°C/400°F/
Gas 6. Tie each ribbon into a loose knot
and place on the prepared baking
sheets, spacing them well apart. Cover
with oiled clear film (plastic wrap) and
leave in a warm place for 10–15 minutes.
Either leave the picos plain or brush
with water and sprinkle with salt or
sesame seeds. Bake for 10–15 minutes.

CASHEW AND OLIVE SCROLLS

*These attractively shaped rolls have a crunchy texture and ooze with the
flavours of olives and fresh herbs.*

140ml/5fl oz/⅔ cup milk
120ml/4fl oz/½ cup water
30ml/2 tbsp extra virgin olive oil
450g/1lb/4 cups unbleached strong
white (bread) flour
5ml/1 tsp salt
2.5ml/½ tsp caster (superfine) sugar
7.5ml/1½ tsp easy-blend (rapid-rise)
dried yeast
5ml/1 tsp finely chopped fresh
rosemary or thyme
50g/2oz/½ cup salted cashew nuts,
finely chopped
50g/2oz/½ cup pitted green olives,
finely chopped
45ml/3 tbsp freshly grated Parmesan
cheese, for sprinkling

MAKES 12 ROLLS

1 Pour the milk, water and oil into the
pan. If the instructions for your machine
specify that the yeast is to be placed in
the pan first, reverse the order in which
you add the wet and dry ingredients.

2 Sprinkle in the flour, making sure that
it covers the liquid. Add the salt and
sugar, placing them in separate corners
of the bread pan. Make a small indent in
the centre of the flour, but not down as
far as the liquid, and add the yeast.

3 Set the machine to the dough setting;
use basic raisin dough setting (if
available). Press Start. Add the herbs,
cashew nuts and olives when the
machine beeps. If your machine does
not have this facility, then add these
ingredients about 5 minutes before the
end of the kneading period. Lightly oil
two baking sheets.

4 When the dough cycle has finished,
remove the dough from the machine and
place it on a lightly floured surface.
Knock back (punch down) gently.

5 Divide the dough into 12 pieces of
equal size and cover with oiled clear film
(plastic wrap). Take one piece of dough,
leaving the rest covered. Roll it into a
rope about 23cm/9in long, tapering the
ends. Starting from the middle, shape
the rope into an "S" shape, curling the
ends in to form a neat spiral.

6 Transfer the spiral – or scroll – to a
prepared baking sheet. Make 11 more
scrolls in the same way. Cover with
oiled clear film and leave to rise in a
warm place for 30 minutes, or until
doubled in size.

7 Meanwhile, preheat the oven to 200°C/
400°F/Gas 6. Sprinkle the rolls with
Parmesan cheese and bake them for
18–20 minutes, or until risen and golden.
Turn out on to a wire rack to cool.

HAM AND CHEESE CROISSANTS

The crispy layers of yeast pastry melt in your mouth to reveal a cheese and ham filling. Serve the croissants freshly baked and still warm.

115ml/4fl oz/½ cup milk
30ml/2 tbsp water
1 egg
280g/10oz/2½ cups unbleached strong white (bread) flour
50g/2oz/½ cup fine French plain (all-purpose) flour
5ml/1 tsp salt
15ml/1 tbsp caster (superfine) sugar
25g/1oz/2 tbsp butter, plus
175g/6oz/¾ cup butter, softened
7.5ml/1½ tsp easy-blend (rapid-rise) dried yeast

FOR THE FILLING
175g/6oz Gruyère cheese
70g/2½oz thinly sliced dry cured smoked ham, torn into small pieces
5ml/1 tsp paprika

FOR THE GLAZE
1 egg yolk
15ml/1 tbsp milk

MAKES 12 CROISSANTS

1 Pour the milk, water and egg into the pan. Reverse the order in which you add the wet and dry ingredients, if necessary.

2 Sprinkle in the flours. Place the salt, sugar and 25g/1oz/2 tbsp butter in separate corners. Add the yeast in an indent in the flour. Set the machine to the dough setting; use basic dough setting (if available). Press Start. Shape the softened butter into an oblong block 2cm/¾in thick.

3 When the dough cycle has finished, place the dough on a floured surface and knock back (punch down) gently. Roll out to a rectangle slightly wider than the butter block, and just over twice as long. Place the butter on half the pastry, fold it over and seal, using a rolling pin.

4 Roll out again into a rectangle 2cm/¾in thick, twice as long as it is wide. Fold the top third down, the bottom third up, seal, wrap in clear film (plastic wrap) and chill for 15 minutes. Repeat the rolling, folding and chilling twice more, giving the pastry a quarter turn each time. Wrap and chill for 30 minutes.

5 Lightly oil two baking sheets. Roll out the pastry into a rectangle measuring 52 x 30cm/21 x 12in. Cut into two 15cm/6in strips. Using one strip, measure 15cm/6in along one long edge and 7.5cm/3in along the opposite long edge. Using the 15cm/6in length as the base of your first triangle, cut two diagonal lines to the 7.5cm/3in mark opposite, using a sharp knife. Continue along the strip, cutting six triangles in all. You will end up with two scraps of waste pastry, at either end of the strip. Repeat with the remaining strip.

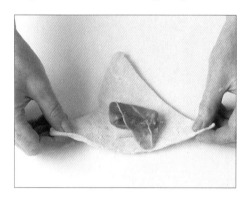

6 Place a pastry triangle with the pointed end facing you. Cut the cheese into thin batons, then divide the cheese and ham into 12 portions and put one portion on the wide end of the triangle. Hold and gently pull each side point to stretch the pastry a little, then roll up the triangle from the filled end with one hand while pulling the remaining point gently towards you with the other hand.

7 Curve the ends of the rolled triangle away from you to make a crescent. Place this on one of the baking sheets, with the point underneath. Fill and shape the remaining croissants. Cover with oiled clear film and leave to rise for 30 minutes, until almost doubled in size. Preheat the oven to 200°C/400°F/Gas 6.

8 Mix the egg yolk and milk for the glaze and brush over the croissants. Bake for 15–20 minutes, until golden. Turn out on to a wire rack. Serve warm.

HAMAN POCKETS

These delicate tricorn-shaped pastries are properly known as Hamantaschel and are traditionally eaten at the Jewish festival of Esther. They can be filled with dried fruits or poppy seeds.

1 Pour the milk and egg into the bread machine pan. However, if the instructions for your machine specify that the easy-blend dried yeast is to be placed in the bread machine pan first, simply reverse the order in which you add the liquid and dry ingredients to the pan.

2 Sprinkle in the flour, making sure that it covers the milk and egg mixture. Add the sugar, salt and butter, placing them in separate corners of the bread pan. Make a small indent in the centre of the flour, but not down as far as the liquid, and add the yeast.

3 Set the bread machine to the dough setting; use basic dough setting (if available). Press Start. Lightly grease two baking sheets.

4 Make the filling. Put the poppy seeds in a heatproof bowl, pour over boiling water to cover and leave to cool. Drain thoroughly through a fine strainer. Melt 15g/½oz/1 tbsp of the butter in a small pan, add the poppy seeds and cook, stirring, for 1–2 minutes. Remove from the heat and stir in the ground almonds, honey, mixed peel and sultanas. Cool.

5 When the dough cycle has finished, place the dough on a lightly floured surface. Knock back (punch down) gently and then shape it into a ball.

6 Roll out the pastry to a thickness of about 5mm/¼in. Cut out 10cm/4in rounds using a plain cutter, re-rolling the trimmings as necessary. Then melt the remaining butter.

100ml/3½fl oz/7 tbsp milk
1 egg
250g/9oz/2¼ cups unbleached strong white (bread) flour
25g/1oz/2 tbsp caster (superfine) sugar
2.5ml/½ tsp salt
25g/1oz/2 tbsp butter, melted
5ml/1 tsp easy-blend (rapid-rise) dried yeast
beaten egg, to glaze

FOR THE FILLING
50g/2oz/4 tbsp poppy seeds
40g/1½oz/3 tbsp butter
25g/1oz/¼ cup ground almonds
15ml/1 tbsp clear honey
15ml/1 tbsp chopped mixed (candied) peel
15ml/1 tbsp sultanas (golden raisins), chopped

MAKES 10–12 PASTRIES

7 Brush each round of dough with the melted butter and place a spoonful of filling in the centre. Bring up the edges over the filling to make tricorn shapes, leaving a little of the filling showing. Transfer the shaped pastries to the prepared baking sheets, cover them with oiled clear film (plastic wrap) and leave them to rise for 30 minutes or until doubled in size.

8 Preheat the oven to 190°C/375°F/ Gas 5. Brush the pastries with the beaten egg and bake for 15 minutes, or until golden. Turn out on to a wire rack.

VARIATION
Chopped ready-to-eat prunes can be used instead of poppy seeds.

SWEET BREADS AND
YEAST CAKES

Fresh fruit-flavoured loaves and rich yeast cakes flavoured with dried fruits or chocolate

are all part of this diverse range of breads. A bread machine is the perfect tool for mixing

and proving the rich doughs of Continental specialities, often prepared for special occasions.

SMALL
75ml/5 tbsp water
75ml/5 tbsp milk
1 egg
325g/11½oz/scant 3 cups unbleached
strong white (bread) flour,
plus 30ml/2 tbsp
25g/1oz/¼ cup coarse oatmeal
5ml/1 tsp ground mixed
(apple pie) spice
40g/1½oz/3 tbsp caster (superfine)
sugar
2.5ml/½ tsp salt
25g/1oz/2 tbsp butter
5ml/1 tsp easy-blend (rapid-rise)
dried yeast
50g/2oz/½ cup blueberries

MEDIUM
110ml/scant 4 fl oz/scant ½ cup water
120ml/4fl oz/½ cup milk
1 egg
450g/1lb/4 cups unbleached strong
white flour, plus 30ml/2 tbsp
50g/2oz/½ cup coarse oatmeal
7.5ml/1½ tsp ground mixed spice
50g/2oz/¼ cup caster sugar
3.5ml/¾ tsp salt
40g/1½oz/3 tbsp butter
7.5ml/1½ tsp easy-blend dried yeast
75g/3oz/¾ cup blueberries

LARGE
140ml/5fl oz/scant ⅔ cup water
150ml/5fl oz/⅔ cup milk
2 eggs
625g/1lb 6oz/5½ cups unbleached
strong white flour,
plus 30ml/2 tbsp
50g/2oz/½ cup coarse oatmeal
10ml/2 tsp ground mixed spice
65g/2½oz/5 tbsp caster sugar
3.5ml/¾ tsp salt
50g/2oz/¼ cup butter
10ml/2 tsp easy-blend dried yeast
100g/3½oz/scant 1 cup blueberries

MAKES 1 LOAF

COOK'S TIP
Use the light crust setting if your
bread machine produces a rich, fairly
dark crust in a sweet loaf.

BLUEBERRY AND OATMEAL BREAD

The blueberries add a subtle fruitiness to this loaf, while the oatmeal contributes texture and a nutty flavour. This is best eaten on the day it is baked, which shouldn't be a problem.

1 Pour the water, milk and egg(s) into the bread machine pan. If the instructions for your machine specify that the yeast is to be placed in the pan first, reverse the order in which you add the liquid and dry ingredients.

2 Sprinkle in the flour, making sure it covers the liquid. Add the oatmeal and spice. Add the sugar, salt and butter in separate corners. Make a small indent in the centre of the flour, but not down as far as the liquid, and add the yeast.

3 Set the bread machine to the basic/normal setting, with raisin setting (if available), medium crust. Press Start. Toss the berries with the extra flour to coat. Add to the dough when the machine beeps, or after the first kneading.

4 Remove the bread from the pan at the end of the baking cycle and turn out on to a wire rack to cool.

CRANBERRY AND ORANGE BREAD

The distinctive tart flavour of cranberries is intensified when these American fruits are dried. They combine well here with orange rind and pecan nuts.

1 Pour the water, orange juice and egg(s) into the bread machine pan. If the instructions for your machine specify that the yeast is to be placed in the pan first, reverse the order in which you add the liquid and dry ingredients.

2 Sprinkle in the flour, making sure that it covers the water. Add the skimmed milk powder. Place the sugar, salt and butter in separate corners of the bread pan. Make a small indent in the centre of the flour, but not down as far as the liquid, and add the yeast.

3 Set the bread machine to the basic/ normal setting, with raisin setting (if available), medium crust. Press Start. Add the orange rind, cranberries and pecan nuts when the machine beeps, or after the first kneading.

4 Remove the bread from the pan at the end of the baking cycle and turn out on to a wire rack. Mix the orange juice and caster sugar in a small pan. Heat, stirring, until the sugar dissolves, then boil until syrupy. Brush the syrup over the loaf and leave to cool.

SMALL
70ml/2½ fl oz/scant 5 tbsp water
80ml/scant 3 fl oz/⅓ cup orange juice
1 egg
375g/13oz/3¼ cups unbleached strong white (bread) flour
15ml/1 tbsp skimmed milk powder (non fat dry milk)
40g/1½oz/3 tbsp caster (superfine) sugar
2.5ml/½ tsp salt
25g/1oz/2 tbsp butter
5ml/1 tsp easy-blend (rapid-rise) dried yeast
10ml/2 tsp grated orange rind
40g/1½oz/⅓ cup dried cranberries
25g/1oz/¼ cup pecan nuts, chopped
30ml/2 tbsp each orange juice and caster (superfine) sugar, for glazing

MEDIUM
120ml/4fl oz/½ cup water
120ml/4fl oz/½ cup orange juice
1 egg
500g/1lb 2oz/4½ cups unbleached strong white flour
30ml/2 tbsp skimmed milk powder
50g/2oz/¼ cup caster sugar
3.5ml/¾ tsp salt
40g/1½oz/3 tbsp butter
7.5ml/1½ tsp easy-blend dried yeast
15ml/1 tbsp grated orange rind
50g/2oz/scant ½ cup dried cranberries
40g/1½oz/3 tbsp pecan nuts, chopped
30ml/2 tbsp each orange juice and caster sugar, for glazing

LARGE
140ml/5fl oz/scant ⅔ cup water
150ml/5fl oz/⅔ cup orange juice
2 eggs
675g/1½lb/6 cups unbleached strong white flour
45ml/3 tbsp skimmed milk powder
65g/2½oz/5 tbsp caster sugar
5ml/1 tsp salt
50g/2oz/¼ cup butter
7.5ml/1½ tsp easy-blend dried yeast
20ml/4 tsp grated orange rind
75g/3oz/⅔ cup dried cranberries
50g/2oz/½ cup pecan nuts, chopped
30ml/2 tbsp each orange juice and caster (superfine) sugar, for glazing

MAKES 1 LOAF

THREE CHOCOLATE BREAD

If you like chocolate, you'll adore this bread. The recipe suggests three specific types of chocolate, but you can combine your own favourites.

SMALL
150ml/generous 5fl oz/scant
⅔ cup water
1 egg
375g/13oz/3¼ cups unbleached strong
white (bread) flour
15ml/1 tbsp caster (superfine) sugar
2.5ml/½ tsp salt
20g/¾oz/1½ tbsp butter
5ml/1 tsp easy-blend (rapid-rise)
dried yeast
40g/1½oz plain (semisweet) chocolate
with raisins and almonds
40g/1½oz plain (semisweet) chocolate
with ginger
50g/2oz Belgian milk chocolate

MEDIUM
240ml/8½fl oz/generous 1 cup water
1 egg
500g/1lb 2oz/4½ cups unbleached
strong white flour
25g/1oz/2 tbsp caster sugar
5ml/1 tsp salt
25g/1oz/2 tbsp butter
7.5ml/1½ tsp easy-blend dried yeast
50g/2oz plain chocolate with raisins
and almonds
50g/2oz plain chocolate with ginger
75g/3oz Belgian milk chocolate

LARGE
290ml/10¼fl oz/1¼ cups water
2 eggs
675g/1½lb/6 cups unbleached
strong white flour
40g/1½oz/3 tbsp caster sugar
7.5ml/1½ tsp salt
40g/1½oz/3 tbsp butter
7.5ml/1½ tsp easy-blend dried yeast
75g/3oz plain chocolate with raisins
and almonds
75g/3oz plain chocolate with ginger
115g/4oz Belgian milk chocolate

MAKES 1 LOAF

COOK'S TIP
Gradually add the chocolate to the
bread machine pan, making sure that
it is mixing into the dough before
adding more.

1 Pour the water into the bread pan and add the egg(s). If necessary for your machine, reverse the order in which you add the liquid and dry ingredients.

2 Sprinkle over the flour, making sure that it covers the water. Add the sugar, salt and butter, placing them in separate corners of the bread pan. Make a small indent in the centre of the flour; add the easy-blend dried yeast.

3 Set the bread machine to the basic/ normal setting, with raisin setting (if available), medium crust. Press Start. Coarsely chop all the chocolate (it is not necessary to keep them separate). Add when the machine beeps, or after the first kneading (see Cook's Tip).

4 Remove the bread at the end of the baking cycle and turn out on to a wire rack to cool.

LEMON AND MACADAMIA BREAD

Originally from Australia, macadamia nuts were introduced into California and Hawaii about 50 years ago and are now very popular. Their buttery taste combines well with the tangy flavour of the lemon rind and yogurt in this delicious bread.

1 Pour the egg(s), yogurt and milk into the pan. If necessary, reverse the order of adding the wet and dry ingredients.

2 Sprinkle in the flour, making sure that it covers the water. Add the sugar, salt and butter, placing them in separate corners of the bread pan. Make a small indent in the flour, but not down as far as the liquid, and add the yeast.

3 Set the bread machine to the basic/normal setting, with raisin setting (if available), medium crust. Press Start. Add the nuts and lemon rind when the machine beeps, or after the first kneading finishes.

4 Remove the lemon and macadamia bread from the bread pan at the end of the baking cycle and turn out on to a wire rack to cool.

SMALL
1 egg
125ml/4½fl oz/generous ½ cup lemon yogurt
60ml/4 tbsp milk
375g/13oz/3¼ cups unbleached strong white (bread) flour
40g/1½oz/3 tbsp caster (superfine) sugar
2.5ml/½ tsp salt
25g/1oz/2 tbsp butter
5ml/1 tsp easy-blend (rapid-rise) dried yeast
25g/1oz/¼ cup macadamia nuts, chopped
10ml/2 tsp grated lemon rind

MEDIUM
1 egg
175ml/6fl oz/¾ cup lemon yogurt
115ml/4fl oz/½ cup milk
500g/1lb 2oz/4½ cups unbleached strong white flour
50g/2oz/¼ cup caster sugar
3.5ml/¾tsp salt
40g/1½oz/3 tbsp butter
7.5ml/1½ tsp easy-blend dried yeast
40g/1½oz/⅓ cup macadamia nuts, chopped
15ml/1 tbsp grated lemon rind

LARGE
2 eggs
200ml/7fl oz/⅞ cup lemon yogurt
115ml/4fl oz/½ cup milk
675g/1½lb/6 cups unbleached strong white flour
65g/2½oz/5 tbsp caster sugar
5ml/1 tsp salt
50g/2oz/¼ cup butter
7.5ml/1½ tsp easy-blend dried yeast
50g/2oz/½ cup macadamia nuts, chopped
20ml/4 tsp grated lemon rind

MAKES 1 LOAF

COOK'S TIP
Select light crust setting if your bread machine tends to produce a rich crust when you make a sweet bread.

SWISS PEAR AND REDCURRANT TART

Juicy pears and redcurrants in a nutmeg cream custard provide an unforgettable filling for this Swiss tart.

85ml/3fl oz/⅜ cup milk
1 egg
225g/8oz/2 cups unbleached strong white (bread) flour
2.5ml/½ tsp salt
25g/1oz/2 tbsp caster (superfine) sugar
25g/1oz/2 tbsp butter, melted
5ml/1 tsp easy-blend (rapid-rise) dried yeast
icing (confectioners') sugar, for dusting

FOR THE FILLING
120ml/4fl oz/½ cup single (light) cream
2 eggs
25g/1oz/2 tbsp caster (superfine) sugar
2.5ml/½ tsp freshly grated nutmeg
3 pears, peeled, halved and cored
50g/2oz/⅓ cup redcurrants

SERVES 6–8

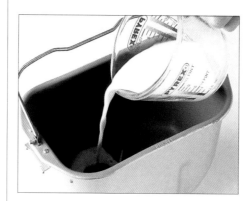

1 Pour the milk and egg into the bread machine pan. If the instructions for your bread machine specify it, reverse the order in which you add the liquid and dry ingredients.

2 Sprinkle in the flour, making sure that it covers the liquid completely. Add the salt, sugar and butter, placing them in separate corners of the bread pan. Make a small indent in the centre of the flour, but not down as far as the liquid, and add the yeast.

3 Set the bread machine to the dough setting; use basic dough setting (if available). Press Start. Lightly oil a 25cm/10in pizza pan, shallow pie or flan tin (pan).

4 When the dough cycle has finished, remove the dough from the machine and place it on a lightly floured surface. Knock back (punch down) gently.

5 Roll out the dough to a 28cm/11in round. Place it in the oiled pizza pan or pie or flan tin. With your fingers, press the dough outwards and upwards so that it covers the base and sides of the tin evenly. Then preheat the oven to 190°C/375°F/Gas 5.

6 Make the filling by beating the cream with the eggs, sugar and nutmeg in a bowl. Pour it into the dough-lined tin, then arrange the pears on top, placing them cut side down. Sprinkle the redcurrants in the centre.

7 Bake the tart for 35–40 minutes, or until the filling has set and the crust is golden. Let it cool for a few minutes in the tin, then sprinkle it with sugar. Cut it into wedges and serve immediately.

APRICOT AND VANILLA SLICES

Fresh apricots are perfect for these fruit slices, but there's no need to deny yourself when they are out of season. Just use well-drained canned ones.

115ml/4fl oz/½ cup water
225g/8oz/2 cups unbleached strong white (bread) flour
2.5ml/½ tsp salt
25g/1oz/2 tbsp caster (superfine) sugar
25g/1oz/2 tbsp butter, melted
5ml/1 tsp easy-blend (rapid-rise) dried yeast

FOR THE FILLING
40g/1½oz/3 tbsp caster (superfine) sugar
15ml/1 tbsp cornflour (cornstarch)
140g/5oz/⅔ cup mascarpone cheese
175g/6oz/¾ cup curd (farmer's) cheese
2 eggs, lightly beaten
2.5ml/½ tsp vanilla essence (extract)
30ml/2 tbsp apricot conserve
9 apricots, halved and stoned (pitted)

MAKES ABOUT 14 CAKES

VARIATION
These taste just as good when made with fresh nectarines. Use raspberry jam instead of the apricot conserve.

1 Pour the water into the bread machine pan. If the instructions for your bread machine specify that the yeast is to be placed in the pan first, simply reverse the order in which you add the liquid and dry ingredients.

2 Sprinkle in the flour, making sure that it covers the water. Add the salt, sugar and butter, placing them in separate corners of the bread pan.

3 Make a small indent in the centre of the flour, but not down as far as the liquid underneath, and add the yeast.

4 Set the bread machine to the dough setting; use basic dough setting (if available). Press Start. Oil a 33 x 20cm/ 13 x 8in Swiss (jelly) roll tin (pan).

5 When the dough cycle has finished, remove the dough from the machine and place it on a lightly floured surface.

6 Knock back (punch down) gently, then roll out to a rectangle, measuring 35 x 23cm/14 x 9in. Lift it on to the Swiss roll tin. Using your fingers, press the dough outwards and upwards so that it covers the base and sides of the tin evenly. Cover with oiled clear film (plastic wrap). Set aside.

7 Preheat the oven to 200°C/400°F/ Gas 6. Make the filling. Mix the sugar and cornflour in a small bowl. Put the mascarpone and curd cheese into a large bowl and beat in the sugar mixture, then the eggs and vanilla.

8 Spread the apricot conserve evenly over the base of the dough, then spread the vanilla mixture on top. Arrange the apricots over the filling, placing them cut side down.

9 Bake for 25–30 minutes, or until the filling is set and the dough has risen and is golden. Leave to cool slightly before cutting into slices. Serve warm.

100ml/3½fl oz/7 tbsp milk
1 egg
250g/9oz/2¼ cups unbleached strong
white (bread) flour
2.5ml/½ tsp salt
40g/1½oz/3 tbsp caster (superfine) sugar
25g/1oz/2 tbsp butter, melted
5ml/1 tsp easy-blend (rapid-rise)
dried yeast
4 peaches, halved and stoned (pitted)

FOR THE TOPPING
75g/3oz/¾ cup plain (all-purpose) flour
40g/1½oz/⅓ cup ground almonds
50g/2oz/¼ cup butter, diced
and softened
40g/1½oz/4 tbsp caster (superfine) sugar
5ml/1 tsp ground cinnamon

SERVES 8

PEACH STREUSELKUCHEN

This peach-filled German yeast cake is finished with a crunchy almond and cinnamon topping which is quite irresistible.

1 Pour the milk and egg into the bread pan. If the instructions for your bread machine specify that the yeast should go in first, reverse the order of wet and dry ingredients.

2 Sprinkle in the flour, making sure that it covers the milk and egg completely. Then add the salt, sugar and butter, placing them in three separate corners of the bread pan. Make a small indent in the centre of the flour, but not down as far as the liquid, and add the easy-blend dried yeast.

3 Set the bread machine to the dough setting; use basic dough setting (if available). Press Start. Lightly oil a 25cm/10in springform cake tin (pan).

4 When the dough cycle has finished, remove the dough from the pan and place it on a lightly floured surface. Knock back (punch down) gently. Roll out to fit the tin. Ease it into position.

5 Slice the peaches thickly and arrange them on top of the dough. Next, make the topping. Rub the flour, ground almonds and butter together until the mixture resembles coarse breadcrumbs. Stir in the caster sugar and cinnamon. Sprinkle the topping over the peaches.

6 Cover the dough with lightly oiled clear film (plastic wrap) and leave in a warm place for about 20–25 minutes, to rise slightly. Meanwhile, preheat the oven to 190°C/375°F/Gas 5.

7 Bake the cake for 25–30 minutes, or until evenly golden. Leave it to cool in the tin for a few minutes and serve warm, or turn out on to a wire rack to cool completely.

BAVARIAN PLUM CAKE

As this bakes, the juices from the plums trickle through to the base, making a deliciously succulent, fruity cake. Serve it with coffee or as a dessert with crème fraîche or ice cream.

90ml/6 tbsp milk
1 egg
225g/8oz/2 cups unbleached strong white (bread) flour
5ml/1 tsp ground cinnamon
2.5ml/½ tsp salt
40g/1½oz/3 tbsp caster (superfine) sugar
25g/1oz/2 tbsp butter, melted
5ml/1 tsp easy-blend (rapid-rise) dried yeast
675g/1½lb plums
icing (confectioners') sugar, for dusting

SERVES 8

1 Pour the milk into the bread machine pan and add the egg. If the instructions for your machine specify that the yeast is to be placed in the pan first, simply reverse the order in which you add the liquid and dry ingredients.

VARIATION

Replace the plums with apple wedges or nectarine slices. Use eating apples as cooking apples will be too tart. Allow four to five depending on their size. Sprinkle the top with demerara (raw) sugar 5 minutes before the end of baking, and return to the oven.

2 Sprinkle in the flour, making sure that it covers the milk and egg completely. Add the ground cinnamon. Place the salt, sugar and butter in separate corners of the bread pan.

3 Make a small indent in the centre of the flour, but not down as far as the liquid, and add the yeast.

4 Set the bread machine to the dough setting (the basic dough setting, if available). Press Start. Lightly oil a 27 x 18cm/10½ x 7in rectangular baking tin (pan) that is about 4cm/1½in deep.

5 When the dough cycle has finished, remove the dough from the machine and place it on a lightly floured surface. Knock back (punch down) gently, then roll it out to fit the tin. Using your fingertips, ease it into position.

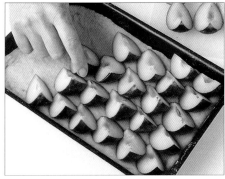

6 Cut the plums into quarters and remove the stones (pits). Arrange them on the dough, so that they overlap slightly. Cover with lightly oiled clear film (plastic wrap) and leave in a warm place for 30–45 minutes. Meanwhile, preheat the oven to 190°C/375°F/Gas 5.

7 Bake the cake for 30–35 minutes, or until golden and well risen. Dust with icing sugar and serve warm.

FINNISH FESTIVE WREATH

This traditional sweet bread, enriched with egg and delicately scented with saffron and cardamom, is called pulla in its native Finland. For festive occasions, elaborately shaped versions of the bread, like this pretty wreath, are prepared.

5ml/1 tsp saffron threads
200ml/7fl oz/⅞ cup milk
2 eggs
500g/1lb 2oz/4½ cups unbleached strong white (bread) flour
5ml/1 tsp ground cardamom seeds
2.5ml/½ tsp salt
50g/2oz/¼ cup caster (superfine) sugar
55g/2oz/¼ cup butter, melted
5ml/1 tsp easy-blend (rapid-rise) dried yeast

FOR THE GLAZE
1 egg yolk
15ml/1 tbsp water

FOR THE TOPPING
45ml/3 tbsp flaked (sliced) almonds
40g/1½oz/3 tbsp granulated sugar
15ml/1 tbsp rum
15ml/1 tbsp candied lime peel, chopped (optional)

SERVES 8–10

VARIATION
Instead of candied lime peel, other ingredients can be used for the topping, if you like. Try angelica or candied orange peel instead. Glacé (candied) fruits such as cherries or peaches are also good, or you could use dried mango or dried pear.

1 Place the saffron threads in a small mixing bowl. Heat half of the milk in a small pan, pour it over the saffron and leave to infuse (steep) until the milk is at room temperature.

2 Pour the saffron milk into the bread machine pan, then add the remaining milk and the eggs. However, if the instructions for your bread machine specify that the yeast is to be placed in the bread pan first, simply reverse the order in which you add the liquid and dry ingredients.

3 Sprinkle in the flour, making sure that it covers the liquid completely, then add the cardamom seeds.

4 Add the salt, caster sugar and butter, placing them in separate corners of the bread pan. Make a shallow indent in the centre of the flour, but not down as far as the milk and eggs, and add the easy-blend dried yeast.

5 Set the bread machine to the dough setting; use basic dough setting (if available). Press Start. Lightly oil a baking sheet.

6 When the dough cycle has finished, remove the dough from the bread machine pan and place it on a surface that has been lightly floured. Knock back (punch down) gently, then divide it into three equal pieces.

7 Roll each piece of dough into a rope, about 65cm/26in long. Place the ropes lengthways, next to each other, to begin the plait (braid).

8 Starting from the centre, plait the pieces together, working towards yourself and from left to right. Turn the dough around and repeat. Bring the ends of the plait together to form a circular wreath and pinch to seal.

9 Place the wreath on the prepared baking sheet. Cover with lightly oiled clear film (plastic wrap) and leave for 45–60 minutes, or until it has almost doubled in size.

10 Meanwhile, preheat the oven to 190°C/375°F/Gas 5. Make the glaze by mixing the egg yolk and water in a bowl. In a separate bowl, mix the almonds, sugar, rum and peel for the topping. Brush the glaze over the loaf and sprinkle the almond mixture on top.

11 Bake for 20 minutes, then reduce the oven temperature to 180°C/350°F/Gas 4 and bake for 10–15 minutes more, or until the wreath is golden and well risen. Turn out on to wire rack to cool.

30ml/2 tbsp instant coffee powder
140ml/5fl oz/scant ⅔ cup milk
1 egg, plus 2 egg yolks
400g/14oz/3½ cups unbleached strong
white (bread) flour
15ml/1 tbsp (unsweetened)
cocoa powder
5ml/1 tsp ground cinnamon
2.5ml/½ tsp salt
75g/3oz/6 tbsp caster (superfine) sugar
75g/3oz/6 tbsp butter, softened
7.5ml/1½ tsp easy-blend (rapid-rise)
dried yeast
115g/4oz plain (semisweet)
Continental chocolate, chopped
45ml/3 tbsp pine nuts, lightly toasted
melted butter, for glazing

SERVES 8–10

COOK'S TIP
The dough for this bread is quite rich and may require a longer rising time than that provided for by your bread machine. Check the dough at the end of the dough cycle. If it does not appear to have risen very much in the bread pan, leave the dough in the machine, with the machine switched off and the lid closed, for a further 30 minutes to allow it to rise to the required degree.

1 In a small bowl, dissolve the coffee powder in 30ml/2tbsp hot water. Pour the mixture into the bread machine pan and then add the milk, egg and egg yolks. If the instructions for your bread machine specify that the yeast is to be placed in the pan first, simply reverse the order in which you add the liquid and dry ingredients.

MOCHA PANETTONE

Panettone is the traditional Italian Christmas bread from Milan. This tall domed loaf is usually filled with dried fruits; for a change try this coffee-flavoured bread studded with chocolate and pine nuts.

2 Sift the flour and cocoa powder together. Sprinkle the mixture over the liquid, making sure that it is completely covered. Add the ground cinnamon. Place the salt, sugar and butter in separate corners of the bread pan. Make a small indent in the centre of the flour, but not down as far as the liquid, and add the yeast.

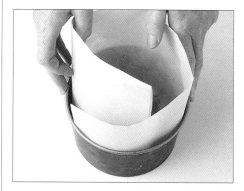

3 Set the bread machine to the dough setting; use basic dough setting (if available). Press Start. Lightly oil a 15cm/6in deep cake tin (pan) or soufflé dish. Using a double sheet of baking parchment that is 7.5cm/3in wider than the depth of the tin or dish, line the container so that the excess paper creates a collar.

4 When the dough cycle has finished, transfer the dough to a lightly floured surface. Knock back (punch down) gently. Gently knead in the chocolate and toasted pine nuts and shape the dough into a ball. Cover with lightly oiled clear film (plastic wrap) and leave it to rest for 5 minutes.

5 Shape the dough into a plump round loaf which has the same diameter as the cake tin or soufflé dish, and place in the base of the container. Cover with oiled clear film and leave the dough to rise in a slightly warm place for 45–60 minutes, or until the dough has almost reached the top of the greaseproof paper collar.

6 Meanwhile, preheat the oven to 200°C/400°F/Gas 6. Brush the top of the loaf with the melted butter and cut a deep cross in the top. Bake the bread for about 10 minutes.

7 Reduce the oven temperature to 180°C/350°F/Gas 4 and continue to bake the panettone for 30–35 minutes more, or until it is evenly golden all over and a metal skewer or toothpick inserted into the centre comes out clean without any crumb sticking to it.

8 Leave the panettone in the tin or dish for 5–10 minutes, then turn out on to a wire rack and leave it until it is quite cold before slicing.

100ml/3½fl oz/7 tbsp milk
4 eggs
225g/8oz/2 cups unbleached strong
white (bread) flour
40g/1½oz/3 tbsp (unsweetened)
cocoa powder
2.5ml/½ tsp salt
25g/1oz/2 tbsp caster (superfine) sugar
100g/3½oz/7 tbsp butter, melted
5ml/1 tsp easy-blend (rapid-rise)
dried yeast
physalis and strawberry leaves,
to decorate

FOR THE SYRUP
115g/4oz/½ cup granulated sugar
75ml/2½fl oz/scant ⅓ cup white wine
45ml/3 tbsp brandy

FOR THE FILLING
150ml/5fl oz/⅔ cup double (heavy)
cream, whipped, or crème fraîche
225g/8oz/2 cups strawberries, halved
115g/4oz/1 cup raspberries

SERVES 6–8

VARIATION
The savarin can be filled with other
fruits, such as grapes, raspberries,
currants, peaches or blackberries.
Alternatively, fill with chantilly cream,
(slightly sweetened, vanilla-flavoured
whipped cream) and sprinkle
chopped nuts over the top.

1 Pour the milk and eggs into the bread
pan. If your machine specifies that the
yeast is to be placed in the pan first,
reverse the order in which you add the
liquid and dry ingredients.

2 Sift the flour and cocoa powder
together. Sprinkle the mixture over the
liquid in the pan, covering it completely.
Place the salt, sugar and butter in
separate corners. Make a shallow indent
in the centre of the flour; add the yeast.

3 Set the machine to the dough setting;
use basic dough setting (if available).
Press Start. Lightly oil a 1.5 litre/2½ pint/
6¼ cup savarin or ring mould.

STRAWBERRY CHOCOLATE SAVARIN
—
*This light spongy cake is soaked in a wine and brandy syrup before being
filled with succulent fresh strawberries to make an exquisite dessert.*

4 When the bread machine has finished
mixing the ingredients, leave it on the
dough setting for 20 minutes, then stop
the machine. Pour the dough mixture
into the prepared mould, cover with
oiled clear film (plastic wrap) and leave
in a warm place for 45–60 minutes, or
until it almost reaches the top of the tin.

5 Meanwhile, preheat the oven to 200°C/
400°F/Gas 6. Bake for 25–30 minutes,
or until the savarin is golden and well
risen. Turn out on to a wire rack to cool,
with a plate beneath the rack.

6 Make the syrup. Place the sugar, wine
and 75ml/2½fl oz/⅓ cup water in a pan.
Heat gently, stirring until the sugar
dissolves. Bring to the boil, then lower the
heat and simmer for 2 minutes. Remove
from the heat and stir in the brandy.

7 Spoon the syrup over the savarin.
Repeat with any syrup which has
collected on the plate. Transfer to a
serving plate and leave to cool. To serve,
fill the centre with the cream or crème
fraîche and top with the strawberries
and raspberries. Decorate with physalis
and strawberry leaves.

PEACH BRANDY BABAS

These light, delicate sponges are moistened with a syrup flavoured with peach brandy before being filled with whipped cream and fruit. You can vary the flavour of the syrup by using orange or coconut liqueur or dark rum.

1 Pour the milk and eggs into the bread pan. If the instructions for your machine specify that the yeast is to be placed in the pan first, reverse the order in which you add the liquid and dry ingredients to the pan.

2 Sprinkle in the flour, making sure that it covers the liquid. Add the cinnamon, then place the salt and sugar in separate corners. Make a small indent in the centre of the flour, but not down as far as the liquid, and add the yeast.

3 Set the bread machine to the dough setting; use basic dough setting (if available). Press Start. Lightly oil eight small savarin tins (pans), each with a diameter of 10cm/4in.

4 When the machine has finished mixing the dough, let the dough cycle continue for a further 15 minutes, then stop the machine and scrape the dough into a large measuring jug (cup). Gradually beat in the melted butter.

5 Half fill the tins with the batter. Cover with lightly oiled clear film (plastic wrap) and leave in a warm place until the batter reaches the tin tops.

6 Meanwhile, preheat the oven to 190°C/375°F/Gas 5. Bake the babas for about 20 minutes, or until they are golden and have risen well. Turn them out on to a wire rack to cool. Slide a large tray under the rack.

7 To make the syrup for the babas, place the granulated sugar and water in a small pan and heat gently, stirring occasionally, until the sugar has dissolved. Bring to the boil and boil hard for 2 minutes without stirring. Remove the syrup from the heat and stir in the peach brandy. Spoon the syrup over the babas. Then scrape up any syrup which has dripped on to the tray with a spatula and repeat the process until all the syrup is absorbed.

8 When the babas are cold, whip the cream, sugar and vanilla essence in a bowl until the cream just forms soft peaks. Fill the babas with the flavoured cream and decorate them with the fresh fruits of your choice.

100ml/3½fl oz/7 tbsp milk
4 eggs
225g/8oz/2 cups unbleached strong white (bread) flour
5ml/1 tsp ground cinnamon
2.5ml/½ tsp salt
25g/1oz/2 tbsp caster (superfine) sugar
5ml/1 tsp easy-blend (rapid-rise) dried yeast
100g/3½oz/7 tbsp butter, melted

FOR THE SYRUP
115g/4oz/½ cup granulated sugar
150ml/5fl oz/⅔ cup water
90ml/6 tbsp peach brandy

FOR THE DECORATION
150ml/5fl oz/⅔ cup double (heavy) cream
15ml/1 tbsp caster (superfine) sugar
3–4 drops vanilla essence (extract)
fresh fruits, such as grapes, star fruit and redcurrants, to decorate

MAKES 8 CAKES

MADEIRA CAKE

Delicately flavoured with vanilla, this classic plain cake has a firm yet light texture. Serve the traditional way with a glass of its namesake.

SMALL
115g/4oz/½ cup butter, cut into pieces
115g/4oz/generous ½ cup caster (superfine) sugar
a few drops of vanilla essence (extract)
125g/4½oz/generous 1 cup self-raising (self-rising) flour
40g/1½oz/6 tbsp plain (all-purpose) flour
2 eggs, lightly beaten
15–30ml/1–2 tbsp milk

MEDIUM
140g/5oz/⅔ cup butter, cut into pieces
140g/5oz/¾ cup caster sugar
1.5ml/¼ tsp vanilla essence
165g/5½oz/generous 1¼ cups self-raising flour
40g/1½oz/6 tbsp plain flour
3 eggs, lightly beaten
15–30ml/1–2 tbsp milk

LARGE
175g/6oz/¾ cup butter, cut into pieces
175g/6oz/⅞ cup caster sugar
1.5ml/¼ tsp vanilla essence
175g/6oz/1½ cups self-raising flour
50g/2oz/½ cup plain flour
3 eggs, lightly beaten
15–30ml/1–2 tbsp milk

MAKES 1 CAKE

1 Remove the kneading blade from the bread pan and then line the base of the pan with baking parchment.

2 Using a wooden spoon, cream the butter and sugar together in a bowl until the mixture is very light and fluffy, then beat in the vanilla essence.

3 Sift the flours together. Gradually beat the eggs into the creamed mixture, beating well after each addition, and adding a little flour if the mixture starts to curdle.

COOK'S TIP
Cakes cooked in a bread pan tend to have browner sides than when cooked conventionally, in an oven, as the cooking element is around the sides of the bread pan. Cakes such as this, which have a high proportion of fat and sugar, need to be watched closely, as the edges will easily overcook.

4 Fold in the remaining flour mixture, using a metal spoon, then add just enough of the milk to give a dropping (pourable) consistency.

5 Spoon the mixture into the prepared bread pan and set the bread machine on the "bake only" setting. Set the timer, if possible, for the recommended time. If, on your bread machine, the minimum time on the "bake only" setting is for longer than the time suggested here, set the timer and check the cake after the shortest recommended time. Bake the small madeira cake for 40–45 minutes, the medium for 45–50 minutes and the large cake for 55–60 minutes.

6 The cake should be well risen and firm to the touch. Test by inserting a skewer or toothpick into the centre of the cake. It should come out clean.

7 Remove the bread pan from the machine. Leave it to stand for about 2–3 minutes, then turn the madeira cake out on to a wire rack to cool.

CRUNCHY PEAR AND CHERRY CAKE

Made from quick all-in-one cake mixture and filled with juicy pears and cherries, this cake has a crunchy sugar topping which contrasts beautifully with the soft crumb.

1 Before using the machine, remove the kneading blade from the bread pan and line the base of the pan with baking parchment.

2 Mix the margarine and caster sugar in a large bowl. Add the eggs, milk, flour and baking powder. Beat together for 1–2 minutes. Fold in the pears, cherries and ginger, using a metal spoon.

3 Spoon the mixture into the prepared pan and sprinkle half the demerara sugar over the top. Set the machine to the "bake only" setting. Set the timer, if possible, for the recommended time. If not, set the timer and check the cake after the shortest recommended time. Bake the small cake for 45–50 minutes, the medium cake for 50–55 minutes and the large cake for 65–70 minutes.

4 Sprinkle the remaining sugar over after 25 minutes if baking the small cake, after 30 minutes if baking the medium cake, and after 35 minutes if baking the large cake.

5 Remove the bread pan from the machine. Leave the cake to stand for 2–3 minutes, then turn out on to a wire rack to cool.

SMALL
75g/3oz/6 tbsp soft margarine
75g/3oz/scant ½ cup caster (superfine) sugar
2 eggs
30ml/2 tbsp milk
170g/6oz/1½ cups plain (all-purpose) flour
7.5ml/1½ tsp baking powder
50g/2oz/½ cup ready-to-eat dried pears, chopped
40g/1½oz/2 tbsp glacé (candied) cherries, quartered
25g/1oz/2 tbsp crystallized (candied) ginger, chopped
22ml/1½ tbsp demerara (raw) sugar

MEDIUM
100g/3½oz/7 tbsp soft margarine
100g/3½oz/½ cup caster sugar
2 eggs
60ml/4 tbsp milk
225g/8oz/2 cups plain flour
10ml/2 tsp baking powder
65g/2½oz/generous ½ cup ready-to-eat dried pears, chopped
65g/2½oz/generous ¼ cup glacé cherries, quartered
40g/1½oz/3 tbsp crystallized ginger, chopped
30ml/2 tbsp demerara sugar

LARGE
140g/5oz/⅔ cup soft margarine
140g/5oz/¾ cup caster sugar
3 eggs
60ml/4 tbsp milk
280g/10oz/2½ cups plain flour
12.5ml/2½ tsp baking powder
75g/3oz/¾ cup ready-to-eat dried pears, chopped
75g/3oz/scant ½ cup glacé cherries, quartered
50g/2oz/4 tbsp crystallized ginger, chopped
30ml/2 tbsp demerara sugar

MAKES 1 CAKE

SMALL
115g/4oz/½ cup butter
115g/4oz/½ cup soft light brown sugar
2 eggs, separated
5ml/1 tsp lemon juice, plus
5ml/1 tsp for the topping
115g/4oz/1 cup self-raising (self-rising) flour
2.5ml/½ tsp baking powder
25g/1oz/¼ cup ground almonds
65g/2½oz/generous ½ cup walnut pieces, chopped
175g/6oz/scant 1¼ cups grated carrot
115g/4oz/½ cup mascarpone cheese
25g/1oz/2 tbsp icing (confectioners') sugar
22ml/1½ tbsp walnut pieces, to decorate

MEDIUM
140g/5oz/scant ⅔ cup butter
140g/5oz/⅔ cup soft light brown sugar
2 eggs, separated
10ml/2 tsp lemon juice, plus
5ml/1 tsp for the topping
15ml/1 tbsp milk
140g/5oz/1¼ cups self-raising flour
3.5ml/¾ tsp baking powder
40g/1½oz/⅓ cup ground almonds
75g/3oz/¾ cup walnut pieces, chopped
200g/7oz/scant 1½ cups grated carrot
140g/5oz/⅔ cup mascarpone cheese
40g/1½oz/3 tbsp icing sugar
30ml/2 tbsp walnut pieces, to decorate

LARGE
175g/6oz/¾ cup butter
175g/6oz/¾ cup soft light brown sugar
3 eggs, separated
15ml/1 tbsp lemon juice, plus
7.5ml/1½ tsp for the topping
175g/6oz/1½ cups self-raising flour
5ml/1 tsp baking powder
50g/2oz/½ cup ground almonds
115g/4oz/1 cup walnut pieces, chopped
225g/8oz/generous 1½ cups grated carrot
175g/6oz/¾ cup mascarpone cheese
40g/1½oz/3 tbsp icing sugar
45ml/3 tbsp walnut pieces, to decorate

MAKES 1 CAKE

PASSION CAKE

Don't be misled into assuming this cake contains passion fruit. It is actually a carrot and walnut cake and a very good one, too. Topped with a tangy lemon cheese icing, it tastes a perfect treat with coffee or tea.

1 Before using the bread machine, remove the kneading blade from the bread pan and line the base of the pan with baking parchment.

2 Place the butter and sugar together in a large mixing bowl and cream until light and fluffy. Beat in the egg yolks, one at a time, then beat in the lemon juice. If making the medium cake, beat in the milk.

3 Sift the flour and baking powder together and fold in. Add the ground almonds and chopped walnut pieces.

4 Meanwhile, whisk the egg whites in a grease-free bowl until stiff.

5 Fold the egg whites into the creamed cake mixture, together with the grated carrot and mix.

6 Spoon the mixture into the prepared bread pan and set the machine to the "bake only" setting. Set the timer, if possible, for the recommended time. If, on your bread machine, the minimum time on the "bake only" setting is for longer than the time suggested here, set the timer and check after the shortest recommended time. Bake the small and the medium cake for 45–50 minutes and the large cake for 65–70 minutes.

7 The passion cake should be well risen and firm to the touch. Test by inserting a skewer or toothpick into the centre of the cake. It should come out clean. If necessary, bake for a few minutes more.

8 Remove the pan from the machine. Leave the cake to stand for 2–3 minutes, then turn out on to a wire rack to cool.

9 To finish the passion cake, beat the mascarpone cheese with the icing sugar and lemon juice. Spread the topping mixture over the top of the cake and sprinkle with the walnut pieces.

COOK'S TIP
If you can't locate mascarpone cheese, use cream cheese instead. It doesn't matter whether it is full-fat or a light cheese.

MIXED FRUIT TEABREAD

When mixed dried fruits are plumped up by being soaked in orange juice before baking, the result is a succulent teabread which keeps well.

SMALL
75g/3oz/½ cup sultanas
(golden raisins)
50g/2oz/⅓ cup raisins
25g/1oz/2 tbsp currants
15g/½oz/1 tbsp cut mixed
(candied) peel
75g/3oz/6 tbsp soft light brown sugar
150ml/5fl oz/⅔ cup orange juice
1 egg, lightly beaten
65g/2½oz/generous ½ cup plain
(all-purpose) white flour
65g/2½oz/generous ½ cup plain
(all-purpose) wholemeal
(whole-wheat) flour
5ml/1 tsp baking powder
1.5ml/¼ tsp ground cinnamon
1.5ml/¼ tsp freshly grated nutmeg

MEDIUM
115g/4oz/⅔ cup sultanas
75g/3oz/½ cup raisins
40g/1½oz/3 tbsp currants
25g/1oz/2 tbsp cut mixed peel
115g/4oz/½ cup soft light brown sugar
200ml/7fl oz/⅞ cup orange juice
1 egg, lightly beaten
90g/3¼oz/generous ¾ cup plain
white flour
90g/3¼oz/generous ¾ cup plain
wholemeal flour
7.5ml/1½ tsp baking powder
2.5ml/½ tsp ground cinnamon
2.5ml/½ tsp freshly grated nutmeg

LARGE
175g/6oz/1 cup sultanas
125g/4½oz/¾ cup raisins
50g/2oz/¼ cup currants
25g/1oz/2 tbsp cut mixed peel
175g/6oz/¾ cup soft light brown sugar
300ml/10½fl oz/generous 1¼ cups
orange juice
1 egg, lightly beaten
115g/4oz/1 cup plain white flour
115g/4oz/1 cup plain wholemeal flour
7.5ml/1½ tsp baking powder
2.5ml/½ tsp ground cinnamon
2.5ml/½ tsp freshly grated nutmeg

MAKES 1 LOAF

1 Place the dried fruit, peel and sugar in a bowl. Pour in the orange juice and leave to soak for 8 hours or overnight.

2 Before using the bread machine, remove the kneading blade from the bread pan and line the base of the pan with baking parchment.

3 Add the egg, both types of flour, the baking powder, and spices to the fruit mixture and beat thoroughly to combine. Spoon the mixture into the prepared bread pan.

4 Set the machine to the "bake only" setting. Set the timer, if possible, for the recommended time. If not, set the timer and check the cake after the recommended time. Bake the small cake for 40–45 minutes, the medium for 55–60 minutes and the large cake for 75–80 minutes. Check after the shortest recommended time. It should be well risen and firm to the touch.

5 Remove the bread pan from the machine. Turn the cake out on to a wire rack after 2–3 minutes.

VANILLA-CHOCOLATE MARBLE CAKE

White and dark chocolate, marbled together, make a cake that tastes as good as it looks. Serve it for tea, or cut it into chunks, mix it with fresh peach slices and add a sprinkling of orange or peach liqueur for an impressive dessert.

1 Remove the blade from the bread pan and line the base with baking parchment. In a separate bowl, cream the butter and sugar together until it becomes light and fluffy. Slowly add the eggs, beating thoroughly. Place half the mixture in another bowl.

2 Place the white chocolate in a heatproof bowl over a pan of simmering water. Stir until the chocolate is melted.

3 Melt the plain chocolate in a separate bowl, in the same way. Stir the white chocolate and the vanilla essence into one bowl of creamed mixture and the plain chocolate into the other. Divide the flour equally between the two bowls and lightly fold it in with a metal spoon.

4 Put alternate spoonfuls of the two mixtures into the prepared bread pan. Use a round-bladed knife to swirl the mixtures together to marble them.

5 Set the bread machine to the "bake only" setting. Set the timer, if possible, for the recommended time. If not, set the timer and check the cake after the shortest recommended time. Bake the small cake for 45–50 minutes, the medium for 50–55 minutes and the large for 65–70 minutes, until well risen.

SMALL
115g/4oz/½ cup butter
115g/4oz/generous ½ cup caster (superfine) sugar
2 eggs, lightly beaten
40g/1½oz white chocolate, broken into pieces
40g/1½oz plain (semisweet) chocolate, broken into pieces
1.5ml/¼ tsp vanilla essence (extract)
175g/6oz/1½ cups self-raising (self-rising) flour
icing (confectioners') sugar and (unsweetened) cocoa powder, for dusting

MEDIUM
125g/4½oz/generous ½ cup butter
125g/4½oz/scant ¾ cup caster sugar
2 eggs, lightly beaten
50g/2oz white chocolate, broken into pieces
50g/2oz plain chocolate, broken into pieces
2.5ml/½ tsp vanilla essence
200g/7oz/1¾ cups self-raising flour
icing sugar and cocoa powder, for dusting

LARGE
200g/7oz/scant 1 cup butter
200g/7oz/1 cup caster sugar
3 eggs, lightly beaten
75g/3oz white chocolate, broken into pieces
75g/3oz plain chocolate, broken into pieces
2.5ml/½ tsp vanilla essence
280g/10oz/2½ cups self-raising flour
icing sugar and cocoa powder, for dusting

MAKES 1 CAKE

6 The cake should be just firm to the touch. Test by inserting a skewer into the centre of the cake. It should come out clean. Remove the pan from the machine. Stand for 2–3 minutes, then turn the cake out on to a wire rack. Dust with icing sugar and cocoa powder and serve in slices or chunks.

SMALL
40g/1½oz/3 tbsp butter
100ml/3½fl oz/7 tbsp clear honey
75g/3oz/¾ cup plain (all-purpose) flour
pinch of salt
5ml/1 tsp baking powder
*2.5ml/½ tsp bicarbonate of soda
(baking soda)*
*2.5ml/½ tsp ground mixed (apple
pie) spice*
*75g/3oz/3¾ cups wholemeal (whole-
wheat) flour*
15ml/1 tbsp milk
1 egg, lightly beaten
*30ml/2 tbsp thick-cut orange
marmalade, to glaze*

MEDIUM
50g/2oz/¼ cup butter
150ml/5fl oz/⅔ cup clear honey
115g/4oz/1 cup plain flour
pinch of salt
7.5ml/1½ tsp baking powder
2.5ml/½ tsp bicarbonate of soda
5ml/1 tsp ground mixed spice
115g/4oz/1 cup wholemeal flour
2 eggs, lightly beaten
*45ml/3 tbsp thick-cut orange
marmalade, to glaze*

LARGE
65g/2½oz/5 tbsp butter
*180ml/6½fl oz/generous ¾ cup clear
honey*
140g/5oz/1¼ cups plain flour
pinch of salt
10ml/2 tsp baking powder
3.5ml/¾ tsp bicarbonate of soda
5ml/1 tsp ground mixed spice
140g/5oz/1¼ cups wholemeal flour
15ml/1 tbsp milk
2 eggs, lightly beaten
*60ml/4 tbsp thick-cut orange
marmalade, to glaze*

MAKES 1 CAKE

1 Before using the bread machine, remove the kneading blade from the bread pan and line the base of the pan with baking parchment.

2 Place the butter and honey in a pan and heat gently, stirring until melted.

HONEY CAKE

If you like the taste of honey, you are sure to love this cake. Serve it with tea or coffee or as a dessert with fresh fruit and crème fraîche.

3 Sift the plain flour, salt, baking powder, bicarbonate of soda and mixed spice into a mixing bowl. Stir in the wholemeal flour.

4 Stir the milk, if using, into the beaten egg, if making the small or large cake. Gradually pour on to the flour mixture, alternately with the honey and butter mixture, beating well after each addition of liquid.

5 Spoon the mixture into the prepared bread pan. Set the bread machine to the "bake only" setting. Set the timer, if possible, for the recommended time. If not, set the timer and check the cake after the shortest recommended time. Bake the small cake for 35–40 minutes, the medium cake for 40–45 minutes and the large cake for 50–55 minutes, or until well risen and firm to the touch.

6 Test by inserting a skewer or toothpick into the centre of the cake. It should come out clean. If necessary, bake the cake for a few minutes more.

7 Remove the pan from the machine. Leave it to stand for 2–3 minutes, then turn the cake out on to a wire rack.

8 Melt the marmalade in a small pan and brush it over the warm cake, to glaze.

SAFFRON PLAITS

Delicately scented and coloured with saffron, these deep-fried plaits are favourite coffee-time treats in Scandinavia.

1 Heat the milk until hot, but not boiling. Pour over the saffron in a bowl. Leave for 45 minutes or until cold.

2 Pour the saffron milk into the bread machine pan, then add the eggs. If the instructions for your machine specify that the yeast is to be placed in the pan first, reverse the order in which you add the liquid and dry ingredients.

3 Sprinkle in the flour, making sure that it covers the saffron milk completely. Add the salt, sugar and butter, placing them in separate corners of the bread machine pan. Make a small indent in the centre of the flour, but do not go down as far as the liquid, and add the easy-blend dried yeast.

4 Set the bread machine to the dough setting; use basic dough setting (if available). Press Start. Lightly oil two baking sheets.

5 When the dough cycle has finished, remove the dough for the saffron plaits from the bread machine and place it on a lightly floured surface. Knock back (punch down) gently, then divide the dough into eight pieces. Cover these with oiled clear film (plastic wrap).

200ml/7fl oz/⅞ cup milk
3.5ml/¾ tsp saffron threads
2 eggs
450g/1lb/4 cups unbleached strong white (bread) flour
2.5ml/½ tsp salt
50g/2oz/¼ cup caster (superfine) sugar
50g/2oz/¼ cup butter
5ml/1 tsp easy-blend (rapid-rise) dried yeast
sunflower oil, for deep-frying
caster (superfine) sugar, for sprinkling

MAKES 8 SWEETBREADS

6 Take one piece of dough, leaving the rest covered, and use a sharp knife to divide it into three. Roll out each small piece into a 20cm/8in rope.

7 Place the ropes next to each other, pinch the ends together and plait (braid) them from left to right. When you reach the other end, press the ends together and tuck them under.

8 Repeat with the remaining portions of dough. Place the plaits on the baking sheets. Cover with oiled clear film and leave in a warm place for 30–45 minutes or until almost doubled in size.

9 Preheat the oil for deep-frying to 180°C/360°F or until a cube of dried bread, added to the oil, turns golden brown in 30–60 seconds.

10 Fry the saffron plaits two at a time for 4–5 minutes, until they are risen and golden. Drain on kitchen paper and sprinkle with caster sugar. Serve warm.

280ml/10fl oz/scant 1¼ cups milk
450g/1lb/4 cups unbleached strong
white (bread) flour
5ml/1 tsp salt
40g/1½oz/3 tbsp caster (superfine) sugar
40g/1½oz/3 tbsp butter
5ml/1 tsp easy-blend (rapid-rise)
dried yeast
50g/2oz/¼ cup currants
50g/2oz/⅓ cup sultanas
(golden raisins)
milk, for glazing

MAKES 8–10 TEACAKES

COOK'S TIP
If you forget to add the fruit when making the dough, don't worry. Just knead it in when you knock the dough back before shaping it.

YORKSHIRE TEACAKES

These fruit-filled tea-time treats are thought to be a refinement of the original medieval manchet or "handbread" – a hand-shaped loaf made without a tin. Serve them split and buttered, either warm from the oven or toasted.

1 Pour the milk into the bread machine pan. If the instructions for your machine specify that the yeast is to be placed in the pan first, then simply reverse the order in which you add the liquid and dry ingredients to the pan.

2 Sprinkle in the flour, making sure that it covers the milk completely. Add the salt, sugar and butter, placing them in separate corners of the bread machine pan. Make a small indent in the centre of the flour, but do not go down as far as the liquid underneath, and pour the easy-blend dried yeast into the hollow.

3 Set the bread machine to the dough setting; use basic raisin dough setting (if available). Press Start. Add the currants and sultanas when the machine beeps. If your machine does not have this facility, simply add the dried fruits 5 minutes before the end of the kneading period.

4 Lightly grease two baking sheets. When the dough cycle has finished, remove the dough from the machine and place it on a lightly floured surface. Knock back (punch down) gently.

5 Divide the dough into eight or ten portions, depending on how large you like your Yorkshire teacakes, and shape into balls. Flatten out each ball into a disc about 1cm/½in thick.

6 Place the discs on the prepared baking sheets, about 2.5cm/1in apart. Cover them with oiled clear film (plastic wrap) and leave in a warm place for about 30–45 minutes, or until they are almost doubled in size. Meanwhile, preheat the oven to 200°C/400°F/Gas 6.

7 Brush the top of each teacake with milk, then bake for 15–18 minutes, or until golden. Turn out on to a wire rack to cool slightly.

8 To serve, split open while still warm and spread with lashings of butter, or let the buns cool, then split and toast them before adding butter.

PIKELETS

—

Pikelets are similar to crumpets, and have the same distinctive holey tops, but crumpets are thicker and are cooked inside a ring, which supports them while they set. Serve pikelets warm with preserves and butter. They are also excellent with soft cheese and smoked salmon.

140ml/5fl oz/⅝ cup water
140ml/5fl oz/⅝ cup milk
15ml/1 tbsp sunflower oil
225g/8oz/2 cups unbleached strong white (bread) flour
5ml/1 tsp salt
5ml/1 tsp caster (superfine) sugar
7.5ml/1½ tsp easy-blend (rapid-rise) dried yeast
1.5ml/¼ tsp bicarbonate of soda (baking soda)
60ml/4 tbsp water
1 egg white

MAKES ABOUT 20 PIKELETS

5 Dissolve the bicarbonate of soda in the remaining water and stir it into the batter. Whisk the egg white in a grease-free bowl until it forms soft peaks, then fold it into the batter.

6 Cover the batter mixture with oiled clear film (plastic wrap) and leave the mixture to rise for 30 minutes. Preheat the oven to 140°C/275°F/Gas 1.

7 Lightly grease a griddle and heat it gently. When it is hot, pour generous tablespoonfuls of batter on to the hot surface, spacing them well apart to allow for spreading, and cook until the tops no longer appear wet and have acquired lots of tiny holes.

8 When the base of each pikelet is golden, turn it over, using a spatula or palette knife, and cook until pale golden.

9 Remove the cooked pikelets and layer them in a folded dishtowel. Place in the oven to keep them warm while you cook the remaining batter. Serve the pikelets immediately.

1 Pour the water into the bread machine pan, then add the milk and sunflower oil. If the instructions for your bread machine specify that the yeast is to be placed in the pan first, reverse the order in which you add the liquid and dry ingredients to the pan.

2 Sprinkle over the strong white flour, making sure that it covers the liquid completely. Add the salt and caster sugar, placing them in separate corners of the bread pan. Make a shallow indent in the centre of the flour, but not down as far as the liquid, and add the easy-blend dried yeast.

3 Set the breadmaking machine to the dough setting; use basic dough setting (if available). Press Start. Then lightly oil two baking sheets.

4 When the dough cycle has finished, carefully lift the bread pan out of the machine and pour the batter for the pikelets into a large mixing bowl.

FOR THE DANISH PASTRY DOUGH
1 egg
75ml/2½fl oz/⅓ cup water
225g/8oz/2 cups unbleached strong
white (bread) flour
2.5ml/½ tsp ground cinnamon
15ml/1 tbsp caster (superfine) sugar
2.5ml/½ tsp salt
125g/4½oz/generous ½ cup
butter, softened
7.5ml/1½ tsp easy-blend (rapid-rise)
dried yeast

FOR THE FILLING AND TOPPING
225g/8oz drained pitted morello
cherries in syrup, plus 15ml/1 tbsp
syrup from the jar or can
25g/1oz/2 tbsp caster (superfine) sugar
15ml/1 tbsp cornflour (cornstarch)
30ml/2 tbsp Kirsch
1 egg, separated
30ml/2 tbsp water
30ml/2 tbsp apricot jam

MAKES 12 PASTRIES

1 Pour the egg and water into the pan. Reverse the order in which you add the liquid and dry ingredients if necessary.

CHERRY FOLDOVERS

Danish pastries are filled with a sweet cherry filling spiked with Kirsch.

2 Sprinkle in the flour and cinnamon, covering the liquid. Add the sugar, salt and 25g/1oz/2 tbsp of the butter, placing them in separate corners. Make a shallow indent in the flour; add the yeast. Set the bread machine to the dough setting; use basic or pizza dough setting (if available). Press Start. When the cycle has finished, remove the dough and place on a lightly floured surface. Knock back (punch down). Roll out to a 1cm/½in thick rectangle.

3 Divide the remaining butter into three and dot one portion over the top two-thirds of the dough, leaving the edges clear. Fold the unbuttered portion of dough over half the buttered area and fold the remaining portion on top. Seal the edges with a rolling pin. Give the dough a quarter turn and repeat the buttering and folding. Wrap the dough in clear film (plastic wrap) and chill for 30 minutes. Repeat the folding and chilling with the remaining butter, then repeat again, without any butter. Wrap and chill the dough for 30 minutes.

4 Make the filling. Put the cherries, cherry syrup, caster sugar, cornflour and Kirsch in a pan and toss. Cook over a medium heat for 3–4 minutes, stirring until thickened. Leave to cool.

5 Roll out the dough to a 40 x 30cm/ 16 x 12in rectangle. Cut into 10cm/4in squares. Place a tablespoon of filling in the middle of each square. Brush one corner of each pastry square with lightly beaten egg white, then bring the opposite corner over to meet it, setting it back slightly to leave some of the cherry filling exposed. Press down to seal.

6 Place the foldovers on lightly greased baking sheets. Cover with oiled clear film and leave to rise for 30 minutes. Preheat the oven to 200°C/400°F/Gas 6.

7 Mix the egg yolk with half the water and brush over the dough. Bake for 15 minutes, or until golden. Mix the jam and remaining water in a pan; heat until warm. Brush over the pastries and turn out on to a wire rack to cool.

1 quantity Danish pastry dough –
see Cherry Foldovers

FOR THE FILLING
40g/1½oz/3 tbsp butter, softened
40g/1½oz/3 tbsp caster (superfine) sugar
2.5ml/½ tsp grated nutmeg
25g/1oz/2 tbsp crystallized
(candied) ginger
25g/1oz/2 tbsp candied orange peel
75g/3oz/½ cup raisins

FOR THE GLAZE AND ICING (FROSTING)
1 egg yolk, beaten with 15ml/
1 tbsp water
30ml/2 tbsp icing (confectioners')
sugar, sifted
15ml/1 tbsp orange juice

MAKES 12 PASTRIES

GINGER AND RAISIN WHIRLS

Tasty spirals of buttery pastry, studded with dried fruit and crystallized ginger.

1 Roll the pastry into a 30 x 23cm/ 12 x 9in rectangle. Cream the butter, sugar and nutmeg together and spread over the dough. Finely chop the ginger and peel. Sprinkle over the dough with the raisins. Lightly oil two baking sheets.

2 Tightly roll up the dough from one long side, as far as the centre. Repeat with the remaining long side, so the two meet at the centre. Brush the edges where the rolls meet with egg glaze.

3 Cut into 12 slices and place, spaced well apart, on the prepared baking sheets. Cover with oiled clear film (plastic wrap) and leave for 30 minutes.

4 Preheat the oven to 200°C/400°F/ Gas 6. Brush the whirls with the egg glaze and bake for 12–15 minutes, or until golden. Turn out on to a wire rack to cool. Mix the icing sugar and orange juice together and use to ice the pastries.

INDEX